The State of the Novel

Blackwell Manifestos

In this new series major critics make timely interventions to address important concepts and subjects, including topics as diverse as, for example: Culture, Race, Religion, History, Society, Geography, Literature, Literary Theory, Shakespeare, Cinema, and Modernism. Written accessibly and with verve and spirit, these books follow no uniform prescription but set out to engage and challenge the broadest range of readers, from undergraduates to postgraduates, university teachers and general readers – all those, in short, interested in ongoing debates and controversies in the humanities and social sciences.

Already Published

The State of the Novel

Britain and Beyond

Dominic Head

A John Wiley & Sons, Ltd., Publication

This edition first published 2008
© 2008 by Dominic Head

Blackwell Publishing was acquired by John Wiley & Sons in February 2007. Blackwell's publishing program has been merged with Wiley's global Scientific, Technical, and Medical business to form Wiley-Blackwell.

Registered Office
John Wiley & Sons Ltd, The Atrium, Southern Gate, Chichester, West Sussex, PO19 8SQ, United Kingdom

Editorial Offices
350 Main Street, Malden, MA 02148-5020, USA
9600 Garsington Road, Oxford, OX4 2DQ, UK
The Atrium, Southern Gate, Chichester, West Sussex, PO19 8SQ, UK

For details of our global editorial offices, for customer services, and for information about how to apply for permission to reuse the copyright material in this book please see our website at www.wiley.com/wiley-blackwell.

Library of Congress Cataloging-in-Publication Data

Head, Dominic.
  The state of the novel : Britain and beyond / Dominic Head.
    p. cm.—(Blackwell manifestos.)
  Includes bibliographical references and index.
  ISBN 978-1-4051-7011-6 (hardcover : alk. paper)—ISBN 978-1-4051-7010-9 (pbk. : alk. paper)
1. English fiction—20th century—History and criticism. 2. English literature—History and criticism—Theory, etc. 3. English fiction—21st century—History and criticism. 4. Globalization in literature.
5. Criticism—Great Britain—History—20th century. 6. Criticism—Great Britain—History—21st century. I. Title.

PR881.H435 2009
823'.91409—dc22

                                        2007052062

A catalogue record for this book is available from the British Library.

Set in 11.5/13.5 Bembo by SPi Publisher Services, Pondicherry, India
Printed and bound in Singapore by C.O.S. Printers Pte Ltd

1   2008

To Felicity and Oliver

Contents

Introduction

This book is about the state of the novel and the state of novel criticism. My primary touchstone is the contemporary novel in Britain; but this is a book written against the backdrop of globalization in various forms, so the discussions inevitably range more widely. The focus is the current state of 'serious literary fiction', the broader literary culture that surrounds and constructs our understanding of that seriousness, and the academic criticism about the novels that emerge from it. The novel remains an important cultural phenomenon, and so it follows that the field of enquiry it generates is worthwhile; yet I am also keen to register a sense of impatience with academic literary criticism, and its deepening insularity. However, there is an equal and reverse feeling of impatience behind the book, concerning the dismissive attitude to academic theorizing about literature sometimes betrayed by literary journalists and novelists. My conviction is that we are often addressing similar issues, although the dialogue that should be opened up by these shared concerns is not always as evident or productive as it might be. Throughout this book I seek to address points where academic debates about the novel intersect with discussions that are happening beyond academe.

A host of questions raised by the processes of globalization will, I hope, make that dialogue seem both necessary and urgent. The economic and social developments from the 1980s onwards repeatedly throw up contentious cultural issues that bear upon everyone's perception of the novel. For example, if academics are habitually concerned with questions of value, literary prize culture now makes

1

the construction of 'serious' fiction a constant matter of public debate. Similarly, the era of postcolonialism makes the internationalization of the novel in English a perennial topic for critics and readers to grapple with. And, most recently, the impact of 9/11 and the subsequent 'war on terror' has had a dramatic effect on the imagination of novelists, while obliging us all to reorient ourselves as global citizens. My aim is to address particular contemporary novels – and particular controversies – that need to be set against the backdrop of these larger global concerns. In the process, I hope to reveal some of the shared interests of contemporary theorists of the novel, cultural commentators and novel consumers.

There are, of course, many forces of globalization at work, and one of the less benign of these helps explain why academic literary criticism has sometimes reinforced the public perception of it as both elitist and irrelevant. I am referring to the logic of specialization in a competitive international field, which inclines 'knowledge' about literature towards a highly insular set of peer-group concerns compromised by questions of professional self-interest. Neither is this the equivalent of those ethical concerns about research in science or technology, where business interests might be suspected of suppressing or exaggerating certain 'discoveries'. For the academic working in the Humanities, the risk of complicity is more nebulous, systemic and without clear origins. Because the Arts and Humanities (certainly in Britain) are regulated by peer-group bodies, the processes of regulation inevitably reflect the interests of those peer groups. Aside from the issue of inadequate funding (which is in any case beyond the control of the regulatory bodies) the material world does not present an obligatory anchor for the academic literary critic, in the way that it does for the scientific researcher (who must show, for example, that this or that laboratory process has empirical results – the inhibition of cancer cells, the reduction of microwave pollution, or whatever).

I am certainly not advocating a more cumbersome form of accountability to the world of industry. Indeed, it is the potential for autonomy – currently under-utilized – that might help revitalize that branch of the cultural intelligentsia that finds its home in university

2

English departments. What is called for is an access of self-consciousness, and a willingness to break out of the systemic institutional straitjacket. The problem has to do with the configuration of the knowledge class to which academics belong, and, in particular, the need for an honest self-evaluation of the situation in which the class is located.[1] I place emphasis, here, on the idea of class formation, or *reformation*, since the self-consciousness I am calling for has a purpose only if members of the knowledge class have the capacity to reorientate their work to reinvigorate its social function. And the need for reinvigoration implies, already, a problem with that social function.

Class formation, of course, brings with it the articulation of class interests. In the case of academic work about cultural topics, those interests have to do with establishing authority, under the sign of professionalism, in pronouncements made about cultural matters. Yet there is an anxiety inherent in that process of establishing authority. The professionalism – and authority – that most academics would want to defend carries a connotation of disinterestedness, an ethical dimension to enquiry that depends upon a sufficient degree of autonomy. Inevitably, however, those class interests have the potential to undermine the principle of disinterested enquiry, and the authority on which it depends.

To particularize, it is in the interests of academic literary critics to generate cultural capital through the work that they do, in the form of their research and publications, and the manner in which this published work informs their teaching. For the purposes of building a career, it is in the interests of these critics to receive validation for, and recognition of, this work through the different forms of appraisal they undergo (and which they also regulate). And it is in this connection that the autonomy of the knowledge class in the university system unravels: outputs are determined by the parameters of appraisal, and the dissemination of knowledge advances a principle of self-serving specialization, rather than disinterested discovery.

What I am calling for, in the spirit of John Frow's account of 'the progressive political potential of the knowledge class', is an understanding of the inevitability of possessing cultural capital in order to make it serve purposes other than personal gain.[2] One of

3

the contradictions that must be grappled with brings us back to that question of insularity, and the impression that academic discussions of literature are, increasingly, the sign of an enclosed professionalism that only rarely speaks to broader cultural debates. Yet it is from the privileged intellectual site of the university that the materials for such a rapprochement might be productively mustered. As Bruce Robbins has it, 'there is no complacency ... in admitting that the privileges of the university are real and sometimes useful, or that they depend on a relation to the outside that is both precarious and politically polyvalent.'[3]

That multiple political relationship brings up another apparently inevitable contradiction for the cultural critic, someone 'without commitment, old or new, to local culture or community'. This 'professionalized intellectual remains estranged, free-floating, cosmo-politan.'[4] The massive challenge is to infuse that sense of distance and cosmopolitanism with more purpose. A new global situation, in fact, obliges academics to reclaim or appropriate the idea of cosmopolit-anism. Such a self-conscious assertion of identity will be a necessary feature of the broader process of claiming autonomy, and seeking to establish authority; and the channel for advancing this project, for the purposes of this book, is a willed encounter with contemporary literary culture beyond academia.

As the opening paragraphs of this introduction suggested, the perception of the academic literary critic as having failed in this regard is not wholly reasonable. Indeed, there are grounds for claim-ing considerable success already; or, at least, for demonstrating that the potential for relevance and meaningful intervention is apparent in the prevailing theoretical concerns of the discipline. It is no exagger-ation to claim that the forms of literary theory that began to appear in the 1970s, and which came to dominate literary studies by the 1990s, revolutionized the study of literature. It became impossible to consider questions of literary value or literary history without also embracing questions of class, race, gender and imperialism. However, the re-evaluation of the canon prompted by this influx of ideas eventually gave rise to the perception that English studies was eating itself, destroying its very object of attention. If there is a germ of truth in this, it is equally true that in this era the discipline established its credentials for embracing globalization, first by extending the canon in the era of postcolonialism, and second by cannibalizing a host of context-based approaches that would make it possible to account for different manifestations of world literature. The tools were assembled to enable literary studies to respond to global change on its own terms.

The contention, here, is that this potential has not been fully realized. One of the paradoxes of literary theory is that, once enshrined in orthodox forms, it can serve to close down the new social possibilities that it ostensibly opens up. The pluralistic impulse to empower suppressed voices can be short-circuited by a normative drive in which a new form of *ex cathedra* judgement is implicit. Indeed, the greatest contradiction of literary theory, despite its egalitarian demolition of the canon of 'Eng Lit', is to supplant it with a *de facto* canon based on preconceived political determinants. Sometimes, however, those political determinants have been so austere as to render the singular literary response insignificant if not invalid. In some varieties of academic novel criticism, the emphasis is entirely on critique, rather than appreciation, since the implicit criteria of value that might (say) deliver a postcolonial novel free of the taint of the exotic, or of global capital, are too exacting ever to be realized.

This is a question of emphasis. If the novel is inevitably in a complicitous and ambivalent relationship with the world of commerce, then all readings that are politically orientated are in the business of establishing relative degrees of complicity as part of the process of evaluation. Moreover, this is not simply a matter of reading symptomatically: complicity (as, most memorably, in the case of Martin Amis's *Money*) has become a self-conscious attribute of recent and contemporary fiction, and a deliberate aspect of aesthetic effect. This is where the postmodern and postcolonial novel reveals a worldliness that makes it the historical counterpart of literary theory. It behoves academic critics of the novel, suitably conscious of their own forms of complicity in the generation of cultural capital, and aware of the comparable self-consciousness of the contemporary novelist, to resist the straightforwardly symptomatic reading that

5

implies they can enjoy an unexamined vantage point of judgement. Neither is academic novel criticism reduced, by virtue of this awareness, to a purely subservient role. I do think that criticism of the novel is a *secondary* form of writing, in that it responds to aesthetic objects of attention that can very well exist without being analysed; but the analysis uncovers an alternative and complementary insight, of particular value if it can be brought to bear on concerns that have a general social application.

I am arguing for a critical orientation that can claim a privileged status if its applicability is properly articulated, and its limits understood. A related issue to this argument about the complementarity of novelist and academic critic is that perception about the notional 'general reader' of the novel; for, just as the academic needs to recognize the sophistication of the novelist, fashioning a parallel response to the global context, so should the sophistication of the reader in this context be recognized.

The possibility of the reader's sophistication, another challenge to the assumed authority of the academic critic, is rarely acknowledged. Narrative theory provides a simple example of how academic criticism can appear arrogant in this regard. A received idea, since the era of structuralism, is that personal identity is a relational construct, established through interpersonal encounters and the stories we tell ourselves about who we are. Our identity and our moral being are structured through external narratives, in this argument; and a crucial source of that process of construction for many people is the experience of reading narrative fiction, since they imagine they are bringing their own moral values (actually already established by external narratives) to bear on their judgement of characters, who may also be wrongly perceived as self-contained personalities.

The intention behind this kind of theorizing is liberatory. The point is to free novel readers from making moral judgements they wrongly imagine to be independent, to prevent them from making deluded referential connections between novels and the real world, and to make them aware of how their own sense of self may be established through the artificial process of identifying with novel characters: the novel reader, informed by narrative theory, might recognize how their own 'self' is a fabric built from external narratives, and the ideologies hidden within them.

The problem with this is the assumption that the academic critic is necessary to point it out. It may well be that a sense of self for each one of us slowly develops through a process of acculturation, and that the exposure to narrative forms is a key aspect of the process; but that does not mean that 'ordinary general readers' are unaware of the process, or that they are the unwitting receptacles of ideological influence. There are very many intellectually formidable readers beyond academe who, perhaps through a lifetime of reading novels, have trained themselves to respond, if only intuitively, to a range of rhetorical narrative effects. Such readers may find the processes of resisting and succumbing to these effects an integral part of the reading experience; they may also build those bridges between world and novel quite self-consciously, especially in evaluating the construction of character as a notional moral entity – indeed, accepting the conceit that a character in a novel has a moral function within the fiction may be a necessary aspect of receiving a novel.

It is through analysing the construction of characters in novels, as a form of moral debating, that the seasoned novel reader builds his or her complex sense of selfhood, through a lifetime of reading novels. After all, every such reader interprets a novel from a unique perspective. As novel readers, we implicitly bring our previous reading experiences to bear on each fresh encounter with narrative fiction, enlarging our own pool of expertise to produce a databank that is unique to us, and which is conditioned not just by the particular subset of novels we have read, but by the emotional responses we have had to them at particular times, or life stages, and in particular moods.

We all internalize our responses to novels in highly individual ways, ways that may not be fully understood. If we build our sense of self in this way, it is wholly unique, 'constructed' through a cumulative series of narrative encounters that is both individual and unrepeatable, since we change through time. If identity is fashioned in this highly individualistic way, informed by a personalized intellectual history, it would seem to be reasonable to think of it as *internal*, given the legitimate sense of ownership that goes with it.

This calls into question an orthodoxy in narrative theory concerning the putative external construction of the self, and of personal morality. It also suggests that the well-versed novel reader might be at a parallel level of sophistication to the narratologist.

This is not an argument against criticism, but rather a plea that criticism should take due cognisance of the sophistication evident in the novel, and in the expectations placed on readers. The kind of criticism that would then result might stage a dialogue between academic and non-academic enthusiasms. This is a blueprint for a form of criticism that is written neither wholly with nor against the grain, but which is more 'with' than has been customary in the era of literary theory.

This might make us more attuned to the unpredictability of the literary effect, and the ability of the novel to comment in surprising and illuminating ways on its context. In the more optimistic critical accounts, the autonomy of literary culture survives − or transcends − the narrow circumstances of its production. In John Brannigan's conception, for example, 'the role of contemporary English literature' is to engage 'critically and dialogically with the culture it inhabits, with the society from which it is inseparable'. As with literature's role, the role of the critic is far from passive, but it is hedged in with conditions: 'I tell my own stories here of how literature engages with recent history, and those stories are ultimately provisional, critical, and imaginary understandings of the literary productions of postwar England.' I entirely support this emphasis on provisionality; and I think it should lead us to a more qualified understanding of the autonomy enjoyed both by literary production and literary critics, while recognizing the existence and potential of that autonomy.

In concluding his survey, which quite reasonably has been concerned with the literary response to England's 'current crises and anxieties', Brannigan suggests that literature enables us 'to articulate the forms of our oppression, the limits of our understanding, and the imaginative potential for change.' This is possible because literature is 'a mode of cultural authority', but one which is 'also available as a voice for the silenced, and as an imaginative space for dissidence, critique, and reinvention.'[5] An alternative imaginative space, with a social function, is most certainly the realm of the literary; yet the extent of the dissidence, or reinvention such a space makes possible, should not be overstated. Indeed, I wonder whether or not the current state of the novel suggests that the possibilities of social reinvention are considerably diminished: a good deal of contemporary fiction in Britain is written under the sign of 'reaction' rather than of 'reinvention', more a form of commentary than a process of 'making new'.

I do not intend this as a signal of decline, but rather as a way of adjusting expectations about what the novel can achieve. I am very far from subscribing to the 'death of the novel' thesis – as an argument about cultural relevance – though this has persisted, even in the period of supposed literary renaissance in Britain since the 1980s. At the beginning of his survey of contemporary novelists, Peter Childs felt it necessary to address this kind of attack, represented by Andrew Marr's polemical article from 2001, in which he wondered 'if the novel has a life cycle of invention, full expression, and formal decay', concluding that 'the "truths" the novel is best equipped to convey have already been accepted', and that high-quality non-fiction may now be better (and so more significant) than contemporary fiction.[6] John Brockman's influential case for the importance of 'third-culture thinkers', those popularizers of science, seeking to communicate directly with the general public, is perhaps the most persuasive argument that the most important contemporary ideas are being made available through non-fictional forms.[7]

It is necessary, however, to sidestep the oppositional impetus apparent in the death or eclipse of the novel thesis. It may be more appropriate to see arguments about the future of the novel as contributing to a healthy and vibrant cultural process through which the function of the novel is debated. Written narrative fiction is surely coterminous with contemporary civilization, and here there is an area of confusion that is worth pointing out: one reason frequently floated for the imminent death of the novel as a form is that it will surely, and inevitably, soon be superseded by new electronic media. So far, the palmtop library, like the paperless office, has had a false dawn: readers like the interface of the printed book (which is one reason why ebook reading software imitates the physical experience of conventional reading). Yet, in any estimation of the cultural significance of the novel, this is most definitely a red herring. Narrative fiction has the capacity to survive the demise of the book, and to make the technical transition to ebook without any palpable alteration to its technical features and capacities. Of course, the possibilities of hypertext that some writers have experimented with will give another string to the writer's bow; but the myriad forms of novel that we currently recognize – or their equivalents – will doubtless figure in the electronic narrative marketplace of the future.

This also applies to the particular form of narrative fiction that is the chief concern of this book: the 'serious' or 'literary novel' as it is currently constructed and understood. In order to begin the process of focusing that understanding, we should return to the more pertinent aspect of the postwar death of the novel thesis, concerning the perception of its waning cultural relevance. The English novel in particular, prior to the 1980s, has often been characterized as provincial, insular, and dominated by conventional forms of realism, and it is this perception of an essentially uninventive literary scene that, especially in the 1960s and 1970s, gave rise to repeated assertions that the English novel was an exhausted form, in a state of terminal decline. In the standard accounts, English fiction is brought back from the brink by the 'resurgence' of the contemporary novel from the late 1970s onwards.

This idea of a renaissance of the novel, especially in Britain, has become a critical orthodoxy; but it is worth pondering how far this new orthodoxy depends on the old orthodoxy, the death of the novel thesis – or, at least, the widespread acceptance of the exhaustion of British fiction prior to the post-consensus period and the Thatcher revolution. As Jago Morrison perceptively points out, such accounts often hinge on serious blind spots about developments that were already underway in the novel in English, viewed in a more global perspective: African and African-American innovations were already influencing and transforming the novel in Britain and the US, though, if recognized at all, they were seen as marginal trends.[8]

To the extent that the 'literature of exhaustion' account of the novel applies to British fiction of the 1970s, this is a consequence of global economics as much as it is a reflection of creative inertia. Britain was beset by industrial unrest at the height of the international oil crisis of 1973–4; but this was a global recession, and it hit publishing hard. It is interesting, then, to see whether or not the novels that were being published at this time point to a tradition in terminal decline. Some of the novels and novelists that stand out from this period suggest otherwise, for example: J. G. Ballard's *Crash* (1973); Iris Murdoch's *The Black Prince* (1973); J. G. Farrell's *The Siege of Krishnapur* (1973); John Fowles's *The Ebony Tower* (1974); and Buchi Emecheta's *Second-Class Citizen* (1974). If we wish to add an example of the persisting, and much-maligned, genre of English provincial realism to the list, then we can add Stanley Middleton's underrated *Holiday* (1974). The list includes the work of prominent figures, and it embraces new cultural energies and fresh treatments of highly significant topics, including imperialism, migrancy and social deprivation, and the society of visual images. In the case of *The Black Prince*, we have an extended deliberation on the rival claims of the popular and the serious, a topic that has a bearing on any evaluation of the current state of the novel. My point is not to compile a list to rival 1847–8, but simply to point out that, even at its supposed nadir of 1973–4, novelists and publishers in Britain were producing significant works in which the important issues of the day – issues that resonate still – were given arresting treatment. These books are all still worthy of our attention.

It is, of course, the presumed renaissance of the novel in the post-consensus period, coincident with the rise of Thatcherism, that has dominated academic accounts of late twentieth-century fiction in Britain. There are good reasons for detecting a shift, but the academic enthusiasm for a new period of creativity has created an artificial period break. This has also had the effect of confirming the false caricature of the British novel in the 1950s, 1960s and 1970s as parochial and of minimal significance; and this has stripped away a proper sense of historical continuity, which has further fuelled the perennial debate about the health of the novel in Britain, a form perceived by some commentators to be of insubstantial stock, susceptible to withering on the vine.

Broadsheets continue to publish articles that take a dim view of current standards. If the death of the novel is no longer pronounced with the predictable frequency it once was, a diluted version of this thesis has taken hold. In this view, contemporary fiction, assailed by competing and intellectually undemanding forms of entertainment, is undergoing a process of dumbing down. It is not just phenomena such as reality TV or sophisticated computer gaming that force novelists to attend to the broad appeal of their work: publishers, responding to the competition, generate pressure from within the ranks by promoting such things as chick lit, lad lit, and the rise and rise of the celebrity novel. The artefact that is being compromised by such pressures is the 'serious literary novel'.

The serious literary novel is not easy to define. What is meant by this is the kind of book that is shortlisted for literary prizes; which is to say – looking at the evidence accrued – a narrative written in an ongoing humanist tradition that enlarges readers' social, historical or philosophical perceptions by means of the fictional projection of character and circumstance (usually), and/or through linguistic or formal innovation (not usually overtly). In chapter two I consider the extent to which prizes like the Booker play a role in constructing this kind of novel; but I start from the premise that it is, by and large, a cultural form that is worthy of detailed attention.

For many readers, the serious novel is far more than this, becoming a vital form of intellectual nourishment, constitutive of their character. I have already expressed my sanguinity about this process; but a recent broadsheet blast against contemporary fiction articulates concern that the stock of this nourishment is running out. Rod Liddle claims 'most of what I know about the world has been learnt through fiction. ... Further, the novels that gave me the greatest insights were those that were most deliberately difficult and obtuse, often experimental, always introspective and most consciously "literary"; those novels where truly important world events provided nothing more than background hum.' Reading John Updike's *Terrorist* (2006) confirmed for Liddle a general trend, which has seen the novelist's imagination suppressed by the desire to make the novel 'relevant and attuned to the times' and 'shamelessly . . . middlebrow'. Apropos of John Banville's attack on it, Ian McEwan's *Saturday* (2005) is another novel Liddle adduces to illustrate the tendency towards a safe treatment of that which is politically current: 'is McEwan's novel any less shallow and ridiculous than *Bridget Jones's Diary* or the latest Nick Hornby?' he asks.[9]

In chapter four I discuss both *Terrorist* and *Saturday* in an extended discussion of terrorism and the 'post-9/11 novel': there I find *Saturday* more self-consciously unsettling than either Banville or Liddle allow. I also find an anxiety fairly close to the surface of Updike's *Terrorist* that makes it more than the opportunist thriller it seems to be. Even so, Liddle's point about the novel's waning pretensions to *difficulty* deserves attention.

Relevant here is the sharp distinction he makes between serious literary fiction and writers like Helen Fielding and Nick Hornby, and his lament about the drift towards middlebrow mediocrity. It is worth remarking that Hornby upholds the notional distinction between the serious and the middlebrow when he asserts that he could 'never write a literary novel'; yet he is also keen to dismantle, at least partly, the division in book culture between 'two camps, the trashy and the worthwhile, since ' "good" books can provide every bit as much pleasure as "trashy" ones.'[10] This very much depends on one's definition of pleasure, and on the point where the pleasure of pure escapism or entertainment becomes the pleasure of intellectual challenge or growth.

Hornby's own first novel, *High Fidelity* (1995), is an interesting test case. It is anything but difficult, yet it is an original social comedy with a relevance to its times that gives it the kind of resonance enjoyed in an earlier era by Kingsley Amis's *Lucky Jim* (1954), another studiedly 'middlebrow' novel that caught the mood of an age. Hornby is one of those writers who seems to flirt with seriousness, and he has, indeed, been the recipient of literary prizes, including the E. M. Forster Award from the American Academy of Arts and Letters (1999), and the Writers' Writer Award at the Orange Word International Writers' Festival (2003). Yet, as a popular comic author, he clearly does not belong to the elite group of contemporary British novelists, so his own admission – or perhaps assertion is more accurate – that he 'could never write a literary novel' is pertinent; but it is an *assertion* because it is part of his own challenge to the 'two camps' of current literary production that he seeks to merge. In this discussion, what is at stake is the usefulness of the current version of 'literary' fiction that creates the two camps division. How far do we wish to defend this manner of establishing value, and how far would we wish to endorse Hornby's egalitarian impulse, which, carried to its logical conclusion, would generate very different criteria for establishing value than those that currently obtain in literary prize culture?

Before considering the mid-ground identified by Hornby, explicitly in his criticism, and implicitly in his own fiction, we need a model of serious literary fiction to work with. For this purpose, and to establish a worthwhile point of comparison with Hornby, I have chosen John Banville's 2005 Booker winner, *The Sea*. Banville's novel conforms to a recognizable literary 'type', the kind of novel that Iris Murdoch would have called 'crystalline', in which a form of poetic style is cultivated at the expense of the detailed drawing of character. A form of consolation displaces the attempt to grapple with 'reality'; and so, in a sense, art displaces life.[11] For Robert Macfarlane, Banville's characteristically precious style, in the manner of Nabokov, involves him conceiving 'his sentences individually as works of art'; moreover, 'like Nabokov, his fastidious style can be interpreted as a kind of snobbery, or at least a desire to keep the world at arm's length.'[12]

Successful serious fiction, for several generations, has betrayed the kinds of qualities that are distilled in *The Sea*. We are very familiar with novels that foreground their linguistic virtuosity in this way, not in the mode of exaggerated postmodern playfulness, but to reflect in complex ways upon experience – and so, paradoxically, to build a bridge back to reality through the very artfulness that announces the division between World and Book. Such novels have very often been written in the first person, in a confessional style. Without question, this is the contemporary manifestation of Matthew Arnold's idea that literature has come to take the place of religion. *The Sea*, a complex first-person exploration of bereavement, mortality, personal responsibility, and the literary effect – which also works its way towards a revelation that is confessional in its purport – epitomizes what serious fiction has become for an increasingly secular Western readership: an aesthetic means of investigating lived experience through imagined models, and addressing those grand themes – mortality, the ethical life – previously mediated through religion.

An essential ingredient of this seriousness is its low-key self-consciousness, the process by which all 'literary' novelists implicitly evaluate (and stake the claim for) their place in the canon. Pertinent, here, is the literary allusiveness of Banville's novel. (One reviewer found, in addition to the book's mythic allusions, embedded quotations from Yeats, Keats, Milton, Tennyson, Conrad, Shakespeare, Eliot and Stevens.)[13] A related aspect is the tendency to describe the world through a series of tableaux drawn from the masters of painting: Bonnard, Géricault, Vermeer, and so on. However, the sterility – or, at least the want of vitality – of this is also an aspect of Banville's portrait of his narrator, Max Morden, a former art historian.

The effect is to undermine, quite deliberately, the kind of self-conscious allusiveness that is the very stuff of this kind of writing: in effect, Banville, while exploring those topics of grief, allusiveness and responsibility, is also demonstrating the limitations of literary fiction to treat of them in meaningful ways. This is a version of that paradox already noted, that the artifice provides a more invigorated – or the best possible – bridge to reflection on the Real: it is the artifice of narrative and memory, heightened in fiction, that is the true stuff of experience. And what is true of personal memory – it is that which sustains us, even while we may recognize it for the self-serving fiction it is – is also true of that form of literariness that issues in embedded quotation and allusion: it is simultaneously sustaining, yet curiously insular.

Yet, cutting against the self-containment of memory (and the circular business of literary allusion), is the desire to understand external phenomena, one's involvement in the lives of others, an impulse that is integral to Max's return to the seaside village where he spent a holiday in his childhood, but which also determines the novel's narrative shape. Max's desire is also the novelist's desire – for shaping closure. It is this that militates against the sustaining artfulness of both memory and narrative fiction. The novel's key action is the drowning of the two children, the twins Myles and Chloe, whom Max had befriended on his childhood holiday, an event that he links with his discovery of the secret passion harboured by the children's governess, Rose: 'I cannot but speculate that what happened on the day of the strange tide was in some way a consequence of the uncovering of Rose's secret passion. After all, why should I be less susceptible than the next melodramatist to the tale's demand for a neat closing twist?' (p. 235).

Max, believing he had overheard Rose's declaration of love for the twins' father, revealed this to Chloe; a scene of childhood sexual experimentation (involving Max) ensues, and when Rose discovers the children, the twins swim off to their death. Years later, on his return visit, the neat closing twist is duly delivered: the older Rose reveals that her passion had been for the twins' mother, not their father. Initially, this seems to implicate Max in the catastrophe of the drowning, in a way that parallels Briony's complicity in Ian McEwan's *Atonement*: like her, his adolescent misinterpretation of the adult sexual world leads to tragedy. We assume that the instability that results in the drowning is a consequence of Max divulging his discovery about Rose's passion. Yet this assumption is not actually changed by the closing twist. The fact that Rose's orientation was lesbian rather than heterosexual may not have made any difference. Like Max, the novel reveals a need for the illuminating revelation, yet causality is uncertain, hazy.

Published in the same year, Nick Hornby's third novel, *A Long Way Down*, makes for an interesting comparison. This novel was not a contender for the Booker Prize, although his previous novel, *How to be Good* (2001), had made the long list. Even so, *A Long Way Down* announces its gravitas through its subject: suicide. For some critics, however, it was this attempt to graft a philosophical treatment of misery on to his familiar comic style that exposed the limitations of his method, the seriousness undermined by formulaic devices and tics.[14]

16

The novel is narrated from the varying perspectives of the four characters who congregate at the top of a north London tower block, a notorious suicide spot, one New Year's Eve. The chance meeting of this disparate group proves to be their salvation, as they form an unlikely bond that sustains them. There is certainly a degree of levity in the opening pages that seems mismatched to the bleak outlook of the protagonists, and which is consequently unconvincing; yet the humour can deliver moments of hilarity that also reflect on the literary treatment. The best example of this is the characters' short-lived plan to meet as a book group, but only 'to read books by people who'd killed themselves', since 'they were, like, our people'. They don't get further than the first choice, Virginia Woolf, since the unstable adolescent, and invariably aggressive, Jess is typically dismissive: 'I only read like two pages of this book about a lighthouse, but I read enough to know why she killed herself: she killed herself because she couldn't make herself understood.' The group decides 'to have a go at musical suicide instead' (pp. 146–7).

The aborted reading group idea – which was to have embraced Hemingway, Plath and Primo Levi, as well as Woolf (p. 147) – is not the only element of self-consciousness in the novel. Hornby's own anxiety about sentimentality is addressed by a running preoccupation with the populist happy ending: indeed, each of the four characters reflects on the cliché of the propitious felicitous outcome (especially in film), which serves to forestall the reader's expectations (pp. 191, 201, 228, 239). This does read a little bit like Hornby seeking to persuade us that this is not the sentimental book it appears to be, with four strangers, unlikely bedfellows, achieving salvation in a discovered community: the characters, like their creator, are pronounced to be too sophisticated for such populism. If Hornby's cross-section of characters has achieved a new sophistication, however, the effect of that is to establish a new middlebrow benchmark of expectation; and, of course, the central idea of the book is to show that they *do* find salvation in a new community. Sean O'Brien may have some justification when he suggests, sardonically, that 'the "high-concept" premise of the novel could be transferred straight to film, where it would join that repertoire of sentimental, faintly liberal films dominated by Richard Curtis.'[15]

Yet is this slight really justified? In some ways *A Long Way Down* resembles Banville's Booker winner for the year: both are fictional reflections on death, both cultivate a first-person confessional style, both reveal a self-consciousness about their narrative structure. The superficial resemblances suggest, perhaps, the separate ends of a broad spectrum of serious fiction (as it is currently constructed and understood). However, Banville's greater precision with words, as well as his ability to make his ambivalent treatment of narrative and memory simultaneously dubious and enriching, lends *The Sea* the kind of unsettling resonance – about *literary form* as a mode of mediation on the topic of mortality – that is absent from Hornby's more formulaic novel.

How to be Good, Hornby's third novel, also focuses the limits of his seriousness. As with *A Long Way Down*, there is a problem with the narrative voice, which is recognizably Hornby's, 'a voice of apparently inexhaustible and androgynous charm'.[16] This element of androgyny justifies, to a degree, Hornby's decision to write from the perspective of a woman for the first time; but the partial continuity with the previous novels reveals his inability, or perhaps his reluctance, to craft a narrative style that is distinctively fresh.

It is Hornby's announced intention to blur the distinction between the serious and the popular that suggests he may be unwilling to depart too far from the serio-comic form that is his métier. The interview Hornby gave to Robert McCrum, on the promotional trail for *How to be Good*, suggests this view. Responding to McCrum's key question, 'What do you think is the purpose of fiction?', Hornby replies 'first and foremost to entertain'; but he goes on to argue that the affecting of emotions through comedy has a serious purpose not sufficiently recognized: 'making people laugh, that to me is something that has always been amiss in literary fiction, that making people laugh is regarded as somehow not an important job.'[17]

In this novel, Hornby makes comedy of the hopelessness of well-to-do north London lives: the good work of GP Katie Carr, and the Damascene conversion of her husband David, from vitriolic local columnist to zealous campaigner for the deprived and the homeless, are both shown to be inadequate responses to the anomie

18

of contemporary professional life. The bleak ending of the book sees Katie Carr concluding that 'the act of reading' is the only form of personal salvation that has meaning for her (p. 242). Yet the evocation of global warming with which the novel ends raises a shadow of despair that renders their lives fragile and meaningless. Just as she is thinking that her family unit can pull through, in precarious fashion, she catches a glimpse of the night sky, and concludes 'there's nothing out there at all' (p. 244).

In a way, this parallels the impetus of *The Sea*: 'literariness', though vaguely evoked, is all Katie Carr can pit against the overwhelming elements of *force majeure*, which render meaningless the attempts to construct a self that is good, which attempts have been the substance of this comic novel; but, unlike Banville's, Hornby's novel offers no *formal* resistance. Indeed, the closing bleakness is so great as to overshadow what remains of the novel's comic tone: the novel's own form is overwhelmed by the serious topic it grapples with.

A novel from the US that affords an interesting comparison with *How to be Good* is *This Book Will Save Your Life* (2006), by A. M. Homes. This book is also on the cusp of the literary and the popular, written in an engaging – if undemanding – style that secured it a place on Richard and Judy's Book Club list in 2007. Homes's reputation has been built on her ability to anatomize the underbelly of American suburban life, most famously, and controversially, in *The End of Alice* (1996), a treatment of sexual abuse. *This Book Will Save Your Life*, like *How to be Good*, features a protagonist who turns to good works when beset by a mid-life crisis. Consequently, the ironic tone we may hope to hear in the title is muted. Like Hornby's novel (and McEwan's *Saturday*), Homes's novel confronts the embarrassing, difficult, yet hugely important problem of how to treat the question of 'goodness' in privileged, well-to-do Western lives. In short, these are books that confront the basic ethical questions that are familiar, from personal experience, to a significant proportion of novel readers (as well as novelists and academic critics).

The mixed reviews of Homes's book in the British press were determined by the extent to which reviewers were prepared to see this as a fit topic for fiction. One of the projects engaged by the protagonist, Richard Novak, is to help Anhil, the immigrant doughnut seller he befriends, to expand his business. The doughnut motif recalls Raymond Carver's baker in 'A Small Good Thing', and the religious theme of 'breaking bread' in the face of adversity. The reviewers' response to this motif (and to the dust jacket adorned with doughnuts) was polarized: one found the novel 'not unlike a doughnut; an unnourishing dollop of sugary stodge with a hole in the middle where its soul should be';[18] while another found the confection rather more appetizing: 'this book will no more change your life than one of Anhil's doughnuts will but, like those doughnuts, it's packed with unexpected pleasures.'[19]

Like Hornby, Homes was found to be exploring 'the same emotional landscape as a Richard Curtis film';[20] that is, the importance of friendship and personal relations either in contrast to, or in spite of, difficult familial relationships (but not among the poor, though Hornby, to his credit, makes a foray in this direction in *A Long Way Down*). Given, however, that the drift towards the middlebrow is an inevitable aspect of contemporary fiction, the theme of 'goodness' in such fiction, with a focus on interrogating the comfortable echelons of society, seems to me morally sound, a way of highlighting the new, unmapped inequalities on which that drift depends. (When Novak encounters his Malibu neighbour for the first time, he takes him for a tramp, rather then the legendary reclusive writer he actually is.)

There is, however, a curious lack of depth to the novel – what Jessica Olin calls its 'unyieldingly flat affect' – and this is both its strength and its weakness.[21] For a novel set in Los Angeles, in which all key moments are filtered through the clichés of Hollywood, Novak's actions as a Good Samaritan are already contained by recollected images that are pure surface, as when he commences a car chase to foil a kidnapper, or when he bursts in to a private business meeting to confront a corporate bully who has physically attacked his son. In that bizarre scene, at a film agency, ex-President Gerald Ford and actor Harrison Ford are both present, discussing a project to make a film about the Ford presidency. Afterwards, registering the security guards' guns that had been trained on him, and which Novak had been barely conscious of in his paternal anger, the reality of the danger begins to sink in; but not for the reader, au fait with the filmic cliché of the disrupted High-Power meeting.

There is a sense, then, that Novak's good actions are already recontained by the West Coast culture that he is seeking to shake off. This must surely be seen as part of the writing strategy, to create a tension between the depicted lives – in which violence is rife, in which disease takes its toll, in which families are broken apart – and the anodyne misrepresentations of Tinseltown, which create an imprisoning consciousness. This is abundantly clear in the final scene, in which Novak's rented Malibu home is washed away by a landslide, the last event in a series where *force majeure* – earthquake, subsidence, fire – ruptures the privileged but precarious Californian dream.

It is the inability to register this threat adequately that Homes insists on, and does so by making her novel imitate the comfortable mood of her social geography. At the end, Novak is floating on a Styrofoam table, a film prop, waiting to be rescued, talking to his son on a cellphone, who is also watching the event on TV in New York. The rescue helicopter, which is doing the filming, pans/flies away to a fresh disaster, leaving Novak in peril. His son is panicked: 'I can't see you any more', he exclaims. 'I'm here', replies Novak; 'I'll always be here, even when you can't see me, I'm still here' (p. 372). The enigmatic closing line, of course, is more than the prosaic reassurance it represents in context. There is the allusion to the words of Jesus, after the resurrection: 'I am with you always' (Matthew 28:20). This is also the kind of thing parents sometimes wish their children to believe when they are dead, and can no longer care for them. Yet it is also a plea for the reality that persists, submerged, in a world dominated by infotainment. The 'goodness' that obtrudes through the surface of this world is hard to see; and when this novel pushes through its amiability to hint at this subterranean ethical other, it becomes disquieting. It is, however, partly colonized by the meretricious world it would satirize; and it is this particular form of compromised autonomy that puts it on the cusp of the literary and the popular.

21

The purpose of this excursus is not to establish the clear limits of serious fiction, but to illustrate a form of cultural blurring that must be reckoned with. If I were to draw a conclusion it would be that the novels by Hornby and Holmes considered here betray the same ethical concerns, and a comparable self-consciousness to more obviously literary novels; but they do not have the same formal or linguistic capacity to aestheticize those concerns in satisfying and convincing ways, and so perhaps hint at that dividing line that establishes the 'literary'.

The self-consciousness of Holmes, however, extends to an understanding of these limits. Novak's acts as a Good Samaritan (as the media dub him) are either made possible by chance circumstances, or by his impulse to act, almost without thinking; and on at least two occasions, his impulsiveness imperils his own life. The potential glibness of the treatment of this theme – unconditional altruism in the service of a community – is subverted in the novel's ending. Novak's existence, afloat on the Styrofoam table, has been endangered not by any heroic deed, but, apparently, by the subsidence caused by all the leaking septic tanks in the hills of Malibu (p. 370): his career as a do-gooder is (possibly) cut short by the environmental effects of consumption, signified by the effluence of the West Coast residents he has been helping. One purpose of my book might be characterized as an exploration of how far Novak's precarious situation, at the end of *This Book Will Save Your Life*, is a metaphor for the predicament of the novelist, and the critic, grappling with the consequences of globalization.

1

The Post-Consensus
Renaissance?

One of the most problematic critical myths in accounts of twentieth-century British fiction is that 1979 represents a watershed in the fortunes of the novel, with a subsequent renaissance that coincides with the so-called 'Thatcher revolution'. Like all problematic critical myths, this one is partially true, hence the difficulty of revealing the distortions it can produce. The case for a sea-change is put persuasively by James F. English when he explains how British fiction came to be read, within universities, in the context of the multifarious global consequences of postmodernity: neoliberal, relativistic, post-colonial, with the consequence that 'contemporary British fiction could be embraced as the scene of something radically new and decisively more important and vigorous than what had come before'. The causal relationship, here, depends upon the degree to which one accepts that the embrace of free-market global economics, under the sign of Thatcherism, brought with it 'a massive rearrangement of the cultural sector'. English believes in this seismic shift, though he does caution us against 'exaggerating the extent and uniformity of the transformations' in British fiction 'since the late 1970s' given that 'literary fields are always subject to inertia'.[1]

I would want to give greater inflexion to this cautionary note than is customary, though without fully endorsing that pejorative sense of 'inertia'. For example, the key instance cited to illustrate how a new mood of globalization is reflected in the British novel is the

23

new prominence of migrant writers from Commonwealth countries. While the internationalization of the novel in Britain gathered pace through the 1980s and beyond, it was an inevitable consequence of the end of Empire, and a trend that slowly developed from the 1950s onwards. We should also remember the reactionary policies of the Thatcher government – particularly the British Nationality Act of 1981 – that were, in their effects, divisive, and quite opposed to that elusive goal of a vibrant, multicultural society. This is one of the central contradictions of Thatcherism, of course: its opposition, at a human level, to the forces of globalization that drove its economic reforms. Rather than an unfettered explosion of new multicultural energies, there was also the clear sense that those energies were being suppressed and/or channelled into the route of indignant anger (most notably in the work of Salman Rushdie).

Academic critics need to be wary not just of the apparent connection between analyses of postmodernity and globalization, and (supposedly) new, and possibly liberatory, energies in the novel. There is also the risk of overemphasizing the new, and obscuring the link with tradition that continues to anchor literary fiction. If Zadie Smith's *White Teeth* (2000) seemed to march forward under Salman Rushdie's carnivalesque banner, then *On Beauty* (2005), her homage to Forster, and a rewriting of *Howards End*, announced the liberal sentiments that, in some shape or form, continue to govern the possibilities of the novel.

We should also remember that the global recession of the 1970s created the circumstances in which the appearance of a renaissance in the British novel, from the 1980s onwards, could be discerned. This puts a different complexion on the assumption that the post-consensus politics associated with Thatcherism produced angry and inventive fictional interventions on a scale that obliges us to see a new era of literary history. It is certainly possible to find examples to support such a view; but pursuing that line of argument, we should reckon with the paradox that new economic circumstances – the effects of Thatcherite policies, if only locally – created the conditions of possibility in which the *idea* of a literary resurgence took hold. There was an economic boom that lifted the book trade; but there was also a new entrepreneurial spirit that corresponded with the idea that a resurgence of the novel was one way of focusing new social energies. The appeal of new literary identities is always (at least partly) conditioned, in advance, by social and economic circumstances, of course. This does not preclude the possibility of an autonomous voice for the novelist; but it should make us wary of where we look for it, and aware of how far that autonomy is compromised.

If the entrepreneurialism of the Thatcherite age produces an imprisoning effect for the novel writer to negotiate, in which apparent strategies of effective critique may be appropriated, a similar constraint was imposed on academia, where literary theory appeared to foment concepts of dissent – under the signs of carnival, transgression, decolonization and so on – but was rapidly transformed into an instrument of the status quo, the benchmark of a new professionalism, with no vital connection to the realm of praxis. In the introduction, I considered the great potential unleashed by the theoretical revolution in English studies, and the ways in which these intellectual developments chimed with the direction being taken by contemporary literature. Within the academy, however, there was an element of self-delusion about this. From this perspective, the appeal of theory in the 1980s and 1990s has a narrower, professional explanation. In an era when the left-liberal intellectual in Britain was embarrassed by the self-destructive antics of the Labour Party, the embattled position of the Humanities created a climate where that which seemed dissident was welcomed with open arms. In the seminar room, at least, tutors could resist the dominant ideology of individualism, and empower their students with the reading tools to help them root out sexism, classism and racism.

Literary theory, usually taking contextualization as its guiding principle, has been curiously deficient in contextualizing itself. The problem is a lack of self-consciousness, since reading politically under the sign of theory, in the seminar room and in academic publications, failed to address the fact that globalization was rapidly diminishing the opportunities for praxis. Academic critiques of the political inadequacies of individual novelists then become doubly ironic. It is not simply that unreasonable expectations have been made of the novel. More worrying is the self-congratulation that accompanies the process of separating the sheep from the goats, the Carters from the Drabbles: the process becomes an end in itself, a form of quietism dressed up as radicalism.

This was the context in which 'post-consensus' fiction could be invented. The early enthusiasm for theory generated a taste for those writers who seemed to be in concert with it – the Wintersons, Carters and Rushdies – in a clear exaggeration of the relative merits of those writers who could reinforce a critical position that perceived itself as 'political'. A new phase of literary history was rapidly pieced together in such a way as to reflect the interests of those responsible for its articulation. If the account of a literary renaissance thus constructed did identify some important voices, it was also selective, discriminatory, its judgements often out of kilter with the interests and enthusiasms of the reading public. This new phase of professionalization in English studies, in short, had the effect of de-politicizing academic work by driving a wedge between the interests of the professional critic and the notional general reader. A question we need urgently to ask ourselves is whether or not there are certain tramlines of critical thinking that have become habitual, turning the gulf between academic criticism and the broader literary culture into a chasm.

It is that distorted view of literary history that is the most serious consequence of this divergence. The idea of a new renaissance in the novel since the late 1970s/early 1980s draws a false dividing line that consigns the novel between 1950 and 1980 to a marginal status. The fact that the prominent novelists in that earlier period – Wilson, Murdoch, Bradbury, Drabble – are associated with a long liberal tradition in the English novel has tended to reinforce the academic enthusiasm for a notionally more radical political alliance between text and critic in the late twentieth century. Yet the persistence of that liberal tradition, with prominent writers like McEwan and Ishiguro coming out of the Bradbury 'stable', underscores the vulnerability of recent accounts of contemporary fiction.[2] This is an idea that many academics working in the field react to with hostility: it is not an account that tallies with the orthodox view of the post-consensus novel.

The critical problems I am highlighting have all to do with the unavailability of hindsight, but also with the difficulty of casting off the straitjacket of academic professionalism. Wrestling with that garment, my stated aim is to try and establish the current state of the novel as a cultural form, with a particular emphasis on the novel in Britain, but also incorporating some pointed comparisons, especially with fiction in the US. There are, of course, a number of snags with this daunting objective. The first pause for thought follows from the anxiety about the lack of historical distance, the difficult task of striving for currency. Most of the novels I discuss were published in the 1990s or the 'noughties', yet I do also mention earlier novels where it seems necessary to establish the literary context in which particular novels are written, and that attempt to establish historical markers, to the purist, might undermine the notion of critical contemporaneity. Indeed, it is clear that criticism of the contemporary is a logical impossibility in the strictest sense: as soon as a critic begins to write about the 'now' it has eluded his or her grasp and become the 'then' of history. Of course, one can only understand the cultural present through the lens of history, so no study of contemporary literature can afford to jettison the impulse to look back and compare; which means that criticism of the contemporary can sometimes look like literary history, too.

The problem of the time-lag is not so easily answered. By the time this book has gone through the production process (typically, about a year for an academic book) we will be heading towards the end of another decade, and the critical urge to periodize the noughties will already be abroad. Indeed, this kind of process is now happening very rapidly in criticism of contemporary literature: witness the historicizing effort of the essay collection *British Fiction of the 1990s*, edited by Nick Bentley.[3] From our current perspective, that volume identifies themes and preoccupations that seem to be very much 'of' the 1990s – Patricia Waugh's essay on the influence of science is a good example – and it establishes convincing parameters for the study of 'the long nineties', beginning with the collapse of communism in Eastern Europe in 1989, and ending with the attack on America on 11 September 2001.

The idea of 9/11 as a historical marker, an idea that has preoccupied novelists every bit as much as cultural commentators, must be taken seriously. Indeed, chapter four below examines the idea of a post-9/11 literature in detail, and that haunting historical moment is implicitly present in the understanding of the contemporary that this book works with. Moreover, if Ian McEwan is right (following Fred Halliday, and speaking through the thoughts of his character Henry Perowne), that the attack on America in 2001 had 'precipitated a global crisis that would, if we were lucky, take a hundred years to resolve' (pp. 32–3), then the response to 9/11, and its consequences, will surely endure through contemporary writing for some time to come.[4] Even so, 2001 may turn out to be just as misleading a marker as 1979, accurately identifying a shift of cultural mood, but tending to overlook those continuities that may eventually obscure the line in the sand.

The elusive sense of the contemporary invariably outflanks the efforts of the literary historian. That which is 'contemporary' may endure beyond a generation in particular circumstances, though the impression of contemporaneity often depends on hindsight for ratification. The idea of contemporary literary concerns having a longer duration than is sometimes assumed is supported by the simple fact of creative gestation: good novels, like casseroles, can take a long time to cook. I think, here, of Raymond Williams's first novel, *Border Country*, which he began in 1947, but which was not published until 1960, having gone through seven drafts.[5] Its longer historical aspirations are reflected in its structure, which juxtaposes scenes from the narrative present in the 1950s, with episodes from the past, centred on the impact of the General Strike of 1926. Its social drama, however, rooted in the issue of education and class loyalty/betrayal, chimed exactly with a major social (and literary) preoccupation of the 1960s. The example is an extreme one, but it demonstrates how 'contemporary' concerns can be surprisingly long-lived. Indeed, it suggests that novels that are deemed to resonate with a broader mood do so because they have achieved a longer view on a topical theme. It is the newspaper, not the novel, that responds to this year's current affairs.

Probably the biggest snag in any presumption to pronounce, with authority, on the state of the novel, is the selectivity that governs any critical activity that is manageable in practical terms. The sheer volume of material makes an engagement with contemporary writing daunting. Indeed, the novel in English expands exponentially, making it impossible for a single critic to achieve an authoritative overview.

Concerning the novel in Britain, the problem of volume is illustrated by the high number of novels published each year. In his recent survey, Peter Childs puts the figure at '100 new British novels ... each week'.[6] This tallies roughly with Richard Todd's estimate of '4,500 and 7,000 new Booker-eligible fiction titles' appearing 'annually in Britain during the 1980s'.[7] Whatever the precise number, it is far too many for any one critic to process and assimilate. Indeed, if a critic were to spend a lifetime devoted to reading contemporary novels, he or she might hope to become an authority on the output of a single year, but then, when ready to pronounce judgement, our time-frozen critic may no longer be reading works with a contemporary resonance. In the absence of the processes of selection that make life manageable for academics working in earlier periods – who has remained prominent? who is most written about? whose name recurs on the fringes of literary life, and is a likely candidate for resuscitation? – the critic of the contemporary has to use other methods to be able to see the wood for the trees. This is where the discipline looks to be most shaky, since critics must rely on second-hand guidance: novelists' previous form; the selections of broadsheet literary editors and reviewers; and the judgements of literary prize panels. Moreover, we are all reliant on that which precedes these judgements: the inscrutable processes of selection that obtain in the world of publishing and literary agencies.

The fact – and extent – of this mediation needs to be fully acknowledged by critics of contemporary writing, since it makes this branch of criticism truly and indisputably secondary. While it may once have been possible to claim a certain primary status for key and innovative examples of literary theory, theorizing about the contemporary novel can never be said to achieve such a status. This is one reason why complex theoretical accounts of very recent novels are both unusual and unconvincing. The initial reaction they provoke – that a sledgehammer is being taken to a nut (in the absence of ongoing critical debate with which to engage) – yields to this understanding about contemporary criticism: its pretensions to primacy are undermined by its evidently responsive position in relation to a pre-existing literary culture that cannot (yet) be authoritatively challenged or rearticulated. The inevitable complicity between the critic, whether journalist or academic, and the book trade's construction of the literary, conditions all of our judgements.

Consequently, the desire to 'periodize' and categorize in any consideration of contemporary literary history is compromised: we are driven to try and make sense of the literary culture in which we find ourselves, even if our judgements are not just vulnerable to hindsight, but never fully independent. One response to the dilemma is to acknowledge critical partiality, as John Brannigan does when he argues against the periodicity implied in his title, *Orwell to the Present: Literature in England, 1945–2000*: he considers the period since 1945 to be 'too recent to see anything but its diversity and complexity' and 'too diverse and complex to enable us to construct one coherent, meaningful narrative of its literary, cultural or historical events.'[8] Yet the contradictory desire to construct just such a teleological narrative, driven by cause and effect, action and reaction, persists. Neither is it the sole province of the professional critic: the critical reflections of novelists are equally prone to this kind of narrative account, which is the impetus behind the artistic manifesto, driven by a reaction to what has gone before, or the desire to advance the claims of a 'movement'.

A dominant periodizing view, and one that lies behind recent cause-and-effect accounts of contemporary literary history, is summarized in Rubin Rabinovitz's survey of the English novel of the 1950s. Rabinovitz reveals how the dominant mood of reaction against the experiments of the modernists, and the novelists of the 1930s, as well as the reverence for older models of fiction, were advanced in the criticism written by the prominent novelists of the age, including Kingsley Amis, C. P. Snow, Angus Wilson, William Cooper, Pamela Hansford Johnson and John Wain. The traditionalism that Rabinovitz identified as the keynote of the English novel at this time is blamed for a moribund tradition, characterized by

30

a stifling critical mood, and mediocre achievement: 'the novelists of the 1950s have not produced fiction which approaches the quality of the novels of the writers whom they have imitated', he wrote. Moreover, a new kind of professionalism, in which self-interest was enshrined, was adduced as a contributory problem: 'the successful novelist in England becomes, too quickly, part of the literary establishment. Between novels, he supports himself by reviewing for the weeklies and quarterlies and by giving broadcasts over the BBC. All too often, he uses his position as a critic to endorse the type of fiction he himself is writing and to attack those whose approach is different.'[9]

These charges – of the self-interested nature of insider literary culture, as well as the sense of a tradition that pales into insignificance when compared with the achievements of the Victorians, or the modernists – have remained more or less constant in criticism of the British novel since the 1960s. For the novelists of the 1950s, as Rabinovitz points out, nineteenth-century models suited 'their realistic style and their concern with social and moral themes';[10] and this perceived privileging of content over form (to put it crudely), while contributing to a dichotomy that is not necessary, does nevertheless place emphasis on the straightforwardly social role of the novel. Of course, there is a contradiction, here, in that this apparent public interest is compromised by the self-interest of those powerful writers promoting the norm. Yet there is an ideological emphasis, in the reaction against experiment, that puts the interests of the ordinary reader above the technical virtuosity of the writer, and this has had a definitive bearing on one important construction of the novel in Britain since the Second World War.

The realism versus experimentalism debate that has dominated discussion of British fiction, really since the modernist period, shows no signs of abating. For appreciative readers of Andrzej Gasiorek's persuasive demolition of the realism/experimentalism dichotomy, this may seem surprising: has not Gasiorek demonstrated, definitively, that experimental works of fiction invariably depend on realist codes, and that realist novels are very often self-reflexive in the manner of more overtly 'experimental' works?[11] In all but the most iconoclastic and avant-garde fiction, readers can depend on an element of narrative suspense (however scrambled the chronology may be) and be able to invest their empathic engagement in the plight of the characters depicted; and even those writers most enamoured of 'tradition' are drawn to postmodern tricksiness. Margaret Drabble's version of realism, for example, can embrace and survive her highly self-conscious use of an intrusive narrator;[12] and even, in the case of *The Gates of Ivory* (1991), the deliberate deployment of a two-dimensional creation.[13]

It may be, however, that we cannot do without a scale of experimentalism which helps us see which pole, realism or experimentalism, a given writer inclines most towards, or to determine the ways in which different impulses are combined. However, the more drastic notion of a dichotomy persists in critical accounts. Brian Shaffer, for example, begins his survey of the British novel 1950–2000 by identifying 'two divergent paths' or 'two conflicting novelistic "models"' in the response to modernism: 'antimodernist realism' on the one hand and 'postmodernist experimentation' on the other. Shaffer acknowledges that his list of British postmodernists – Martin Amis, Julian Barnes, A. S. Byatt, Angela Carter, John Fowles, Ian McEwan, Salman Rushdie and Graham Swift – must be characterized as 'divergent', given the range of 'formal, linguistic, and thematic' elements in the novels of these writers. Yet he sees these writers as united in their development of the modernist project, and their rejection of the 'antimodernist backlash'.

The problem with enlisting these writers – perhaps any writer – in the name of a postmodernism with a beneficent political underpinning is that to do so implies a uniform ideological conviction about the novel that is unconvincing. Shaffer summarizes the orthodoxy, which many will find highly appealing, very skilfully. In this view, postmodernist writers, faced with a crisis of representation, in which the text becomes more important than the reality to which it alludes, find ways to make this productive. A key element in this new emphasis on textuality is the impulse to blur the distinction between 'high' and 'low' art through the process of quoting from, or alluding to, popular cultural forms. It is 'the postmodernist novel's abundant use of popular cultural discourse' that produces its 'demotic orientation'.

Of course, the anti-modernist backlash, associated most clearly, perhaps, with the Movement of the 1950s, was predicated on a demotic impulse – to make literature intelligible to the ordinary intelligent reader, baffled by the obfuscations of modernist expression. *Midnight's Children*, one of Shaffer's exemplary postmodernist novels, may well have 'stretched the English-language novel, linguistically and structurally' by virtue of its 'myriad interweaving narratives and voices'; but the demotic impulse in this is not immediately discernible.[14] If there is one, it is the (laudable) impulse that presumes the intelligent ordinary reader can cope with complexity and with difficulty; but this is a very different form of populism from Kingsley Amis's blunt attack on Joyce and Woolf, and his championing of a direct, transparent style. The 'populism' of postmodernism, with its expectation that we have all raised our game, hinges on extraneous factors, including the health of the publishing industry, and the growth of an increasingly sophisticated, and increasingly cosmopolitan, readership, produced largely by the expansion of Higher Education in the second half of the twentieth century.

John Fowles is an interesting example of the problems inherent in defining literary postmodernism as having a politically progressive character. *The French Lieutenant's Woman* (1969) is usually hailed as one of the first British postmodernist novels; yet Fowles is not taught as much as he was, a fall from grace now compounded, I suspect, because of the illiberal attitudes expressed in his journals.[15] There is a paradox in the fact of Fowles's unfashionableness, since his work is curiously contemporary in its emphasis on the self. If Hal Jensen is right that 'the type of novel that Fowles kept attempting' is best described as 'a capacious literary-philosophical-autobiographical holdall', then we might see his work as the grandest expression of a current norm, the first-person narrative with a strongly 'confessional' air.[16] It may be the grandness of the design, however, that makes Fowles unwieldy for current tastes.

With respect to the novel, it is obvious enough that the typical manifestation of the twentieth century is both shorter and less socially encompassing than its triple-decker nineteenth-century antecedents. This may indeed signal that the novel is in decline, in a purely aesthetic and qualitative sense, and that it has enjoyed its heyday. This is very much beside the point, however: through the twentieth century, the novel became the principal literary form, emphatically eclipsing poetry and live drama, and it is now the form that is widely held to have the capacity to illuminate our lives by inspiring personal reflection. It is clear that the formal changes to the novel are market-driven, having to do with the mechanics of production and distribution, and with consumer lifestyle. The interesting questions are then: what kind of consumer finds contemporary fiction illuminating, especially where the emphasis is on the confessional individual voice? What kind of consumer, in a fast-paced world, finds the solitary business of novel reading a rewarding experience?

The obvious and simplistic answers to these questions might reveal the novel to be a form of self-therapy for readers, an intellectual escape from the hurly-burly; and, where that commonplace formal emphasis on individual experience is apparent, the contemporary novel might be said to offer a crumb of comfort to the solitary reader: in your isolation, you are not a freak, but joined to the generality.

If, as Ian Watt authoritatively argued fifty years ago, the rise of the English novel coincided with the development of capitalist trade in the seventeenth century, and the ideology of individualism that accompanied a new era of economics, then we should be accustomed to seeing the relationship between ideology, economics and the form of the novel. It is this kind of political embedding that generates the periodizing break commonly identified in the late twentieth-century British novel: if Thatcherism unleashed a new ideology of individualism, in tune with the post-consensus, free-market philosophy of the political scene since 1979, it must have had an impact on the novel. Certainly, there are novels that responded to this new individualism with élan, and satirical anger, like *Money* (1984) by Martin Amis, a comic *tour de force* that ridicules the new social greed and consumerism, most obviously through the egregious narrating persona, John Self. This was Amis's first really substantial novel: it is as if a new form of anti-social individualism (dressed up as entrepreneurialism) gave him the necessary inspiration to forge a new and vital form of satire. Of course, the novel is also deeply (and knowingly) implicated in the

34

effects of the ideology that it would repudiate, but which infiltrates its narrative voice. Indeed, it may be Amis's acknowledgement – and embrace – of this complicity, signalled as an inevitability throughout his work, that gives his novels their particular authority.

Yet such examples, as I have indicated, can be seized upon in such a way as to exaggerate or overstate the 'break', here: Amis's previous novels betray a similar emphasis on individual self-regard, on a smaller scale, much as the disappearance of communal values in British society was well underway before 1979. As with any 'break', *Money*, written in 1981–2, when the impulses of the so-called Thatcher revolution were apparent, arises out of a set of circumstances in which longer-term trends and cross-currents are made manifest. Even so, it is credible to see the emphasis on individual experience, which gathered pace in the twentieth-century novel, put into a more urgent context by the new ideology of individualism. The real value of the phase of British magic realism, in the best work of Carter, Rushdie and then Winterson, may be the gesture to resist this ideology through carnivalesque, and anti-realist, mythic perception. The predominant form taken by serious fiction since the late 1970s, however, betrays the imprint of the new individualism. The series of deluded (and even solipsistic) narrators created by Ian McEwan and Kazuo Ishiguro, for example, must be seen in the context of a society in which communal possibilities are perceived to be fast evaporating: as with Amis, the strategy is to resist that which has also been internalized – for the reader, as for the writer.

This observation reinforces the truism that the literary novel has always been in a paradoxical relationship with the political culture that creates its conditions of possibility. Indeed, one way of defining the literary novel, against more popular forms of fiction, is the greater degree of resistance to the ideological and political status quo: through its structural ambivalences and complicities, the literary novel is the enemy within. What might take us beyond the truism is the extent to which the emphasis on solitary experience in the novel has become pervasive. The cultural niche established by the poetic short novel hinges, perhaps, on its cultivation of that form of isolation that chimes with the post-consensus world, but which also pre-dates that era.

In this view, the literary novel has been forced slowly into a cul-de-sac in which its relevance is dependent upon its complicity. Yet the nature of that complicity may be inevitable; and not, ultimately, disabling.

One reason why this notable strand of novel writing has been pushed into such a cul-de-sac is that novelists can no longer appeal to shared conceptions of typicality in the way that they once did. A consequence of social experience through the twentieth century and beyond is that there is no agreed moral stance, and this makes it difficult to deploy the old-style omniscient narrator, or to embed the experiences of a character in the landscape of shared values. Yet this is also an inevitable consequence of an increasingly pluralistic society, in which previously unheard or silenced voices are expressed. From another perspective, then, the loss of agreed values opens up the possibility of fresh social and cultural exploration.

At the same time, the internalization of the new individualism produces a great many novels in which issues of cultural pluralism and diversity are not the headline issues. Beneath the tip of the iceberg of the novel since 1979, there is a vast body of material that has been largely invisible in the seminar room, and under-represented in the prize culture. The distortion of literary history that has resulted needs to be clearly exposed.

In the rest of this chapter I want to concentrate on a mode of fiction that represents an oblique and resigned response to the society that developed in Britain in the later twentieth century, a mode that is more a form of reaction than reinvention. I am thinking of provincial realism, but more particularly, a sub-genre that borrows from it, the 'seaside novel'. The construction of the post-consensus novel finds no space for the enduring tradition of provincial realism. Yet provincial realism continues to cast a long shadow over British literary culture, however infrequently it may figure on university reading lists. It also has the capacity to illuminate post-consensus society, despite lacking the ostensibly radical formal credentials that are ascribed to postcolonial and postmodern novels. The contemporary manifestation of the seaside novel concentrates the key features of provincial realism, and is implicitly revealing about its social context, in ways that are not immediately apparent.

The seaside, or at least the coastal town, has been a significant presence in the English novel, providing not just a backdrop, but a means of focusing key social relations, as in *Mansfield Park* or *David Copperfield*. For the modernists, the seaside assumed symbolic status, whether linked to the artistic sensibility (Joyce, Proust, Woolf), or in Eliot, portentously, to the anatomy of Western civilization ('On Margate Sands / I can connect / Nothing with nothing'). However, for the British novelist in the later twentieth century and beyond, the seaside became a setting that combined the emblematic aspect of modernist treatments with the capacity of realism to produce a convincing social microcosm. I am especially interested in the development of this genre in the 1990s, which resulted in a form suggesting social representativeness, but without compromising the lonely voice that predominates in late twentieth-century and contemporary fiction: this is a curiously intense form of interiorized social fiction, its effectiveness dependent on what the seaside has come to connote in the collective unconscious.

A key novel in the development of this genre – possibly its ur-text – is Graham Greene's *Brighton Rock* (1938). Greene's despairing examination of the usefulness of faith to counter evil raises a vital question for Western civilization in the light of the rise of Nazism;[17] it also creates an archetypal depiction of the seaside, seedy and rotten, in which the channels of brute power and exploitation are made manifest. It is this established aspect of the seaside setting – as, in effect, intimately connected with other social sites – that gives it its enduring power and utility for the novelist.

Before considering the kind of seaside novel that emerges after Thatcher, I want to examine some earlier examples in this developing tradition. Important, here, is Stanley Middleton's *Holiday* (1974), a novel that exhibits several key features of the genre. Edwin Fisher's 'holiday', returning to the Lincolnshire seaside resort of his childhood summers, is also an escape from his failing marriage, but an escape that is impossible. Indeed, the novel concerns the process of confronting the past as a means to marital reconciliation, a process that is typical of the seaside novel. The seaside is a place associated with reflection, recreation and childhood, and so it assumes the status, not just of an ideal backdrop, but of a seemingly *necessary* location for the first-person confessional exploration that has become so dominant in contemporary writing. Although there are clear religious and mythic resonances in the seaside location, by virtue of water's elemental connection to rituals of birth and death, the seaside novel has assumed its own modern mythic status. It is that modern inflexion of the elegiac novel, in which – in the pervasive context of cultural plural-ism – the uncertain quest for identity is all, that gives the seaside novel part of its curious and unsettling contemporary relevance. I say curious and unsettling because the evocative power I am trying to identify in the seaside novel is predicated on the forced juxtaposition of the conundrum of identity in the narrative present with nostalgia, where nostalgia invokes the personal memories of the traditional British holiday location: an enshrined national myth is exposed to (and by) a context of uncertainty.

If we are right to see the novel's treatment of time as one of its key defining features, then the particular juxtaposition of past and present in the seaside novel becomes still more significant, from a technical point of view. The novel, in predominantly secular societies, makes sense of experience in time. It is a medium designed to imagine, and follow, the notional present in the lives of one or more characters, and to make connections with the 'past' and 'future' experiences in these imagined lives. The special claim that we can make for the novel is that it can produce the effect of time being 'horizontal' – as it is in the way our important memories determine our sense of who we are – rather than simply chronological. Moreover, if contemporary life seems increasingly to be governed by linear 'clock time' – career goals, culture driven by rapid technological advance – then to enter 'the world of the novel' is not simply to escape from the culture of ephemera, but to engage with a form that emulates the 'mythic' mode of thinking that makes us fully human. The novel, in other words, enacts a form of interconnected temporal consciousness that is neces-sary to our existence, but which is largely uncultivated in the routine experience of a secular society.

Thinking about this capacity in relation to the seaside novel suggests a paradox. Here is a type of novel that might, like all novels, provide a way of pondering the psychic basis of social being, even though its setting appears to embody a form of withdrawal from diurnal reality. Before considering some more recent (and obviously 'contemporary') examples, another earlier, and less 'provincial', illustration may help to underscore this surface paradox. I am thinking of Iris Murdoch's *The Sea, The Sea* (1978), a novel that typifies her preoccupation with personal responsibility in a contingent world.

Following the conventions of the seaside genre, *The Sea, The Sea* is a first-person narrative in which the protagonist's predicament, rooted in a recognizable form of identity crisis, is explored after a removal to the coast. Charles Arrowby, a famous man of the theatre (actor, playwright and director), buys a house at the sea's edge, in a gesture of social withdrawal, to write a memoir. Predictably, all the key figures from his past follow him there, and the egotistical Arrowby begins to learn the lesson that withdrawal is impossible, that he has responsibility for his involvement in others' lives.

The benign influence of Arrowby's cousin James, with his Buddhist philosophy, has a direct bearing on the state of calm with which the novel proper ends, Arrowby's personal muddle having been untangled; yet Murdoch, committed as a novelist to the contingent wheel of life, ends the book with a postscript that has Arrowby back in London, about to resume his monstrous, egotistical existence. John Banville's *The Sea*, discussed in the introduction, makes up a triumvirate of Booker winners (alongside Murdoch's novel, and Middleton's *Holiday*) that display some of the essential characteristics of the seaside genre.

Here, however, I am especially concerned with that branch of the contemporary seaside novel, represented more by Middleton than by Murdoch or Banville, in which a prosaic brand of realism evokes a particular place. In the seaside novel, the provincial realism that we more readily associate with the Midlands in postwar fiction – the Leicester of William Cooper, the Nottingham of Middleton – is superimposed on a more elegiac or poetic depiction of coastal experience.

It is intriguing to speculate on the precise context for the development of this school of writing. Given that the novel in Britain is widely assumed to have enjoyed a renaissance in the 1980s, sometimes characterized by the emergence of a British school of magic realism, we might now be able to discern something of a reaction against this phase, or the *construction* of this phase, through the 1990s and beyond. This reaction is characterized by a revitalized form of provincial realism, written by under-recognized novelists including Stephen Blanchard, Andrew Cowan and Chris Paling, all three of whom have found the seaside novel amenable to their purposes.

Blanchard is one of the key exponents of the new provincial realism, his deceptively laconic style representative in its ability to extract great poignancy from (apparently) simple, prosaic description. His second novel, *Wilson's Island* (1997), centres on the return of Ralph, an aimless thirty-something, to his hometown after a period away 'along the coast'. The setting is vague, and Ralph's motivation is unclear: a mood of aimlessness and decrepitude hangs over the book, together with the impression of seediness and small-time gangsterism with which the seaside has become associated in both the popular and the literary imagination: in such instances, there are clear echoes of *Brighton Rock*.

Like many seaside novels, this one uses its setting to concentrate the theme of familial dysfunction, which is exposed more clearly in the absence of humdrum suburban activities and lifestyles. This is a book of makeshift lives, on the social periphery. Ralph's brooding resentment against his father, a dealer in second-hand domestic appliances, dominates the narrative. The father persuades Ralph to lend a hand in the business, and also to apply his talent at playing darts for cash. He has called his father 'Cliff' ever since he abandoned his family for a time when Ralph was little. Another key figure in the book is the grandmother, Ma, or Marion, a fading matriarch who now spends most of her time in bed.

The most powerful element is the recurring motif of Wilson's Island, and the local mythology of something witnessed there long ago. In one version of the story, a naked man was seen on a shed roof; yet there is also a folk memory that something more mystical may have been witnessed, perhaps something with a religious significance. For some characters, the island is imbued with a distant spiritual potential, though this has been submerged in the popular imagination and reduced to something smutty. This is a baldly drawn metaphor for the vacuous lives of the novel's characters; but it works well, because it conveys a form of spiritual bankruptcy, or simply imaginative failure, that chimes with contemporaneous assessments of the seaside town.

In *The Paraffin Child* (1999), we are in familiar Blanchard territory: a seedy seaside town in the north of England with its snooker halls and caravan parks. Protagonist John Drean is a pill-popping taxi driver, struggling to rebuild his life after the disappearance of his four-year-old daughter, Pearl, who went missing in the woods, in the manner of a doomed Little Red Riding Hood. This is a novel of lives arrested by trauma. In the opening scene of this novel dominated by the motif of fire, Drean douses with paraffin and burns all his photographs of his daughter. His self-destructiveness is epitomized in his relationship with Enid, a pyromaniac: in a telling moment, she stubs a cigarette out on Drean's flesh, in the attempt to share with him the language of fire. Fire – and, specifically, paraffin flame – is the book's symbolic motif. Paraffin burns rapidly and nearly invisibly in daylight, evoking, in the manner of Blanchard's understated style, that which is not fully registered at first, but which is still painful and destructive. The run-down seaside is the external correlative of this process of concealed destruction.

The facility with which seaside provincial realism embraces this kind of overarching symbolism is an arresting feature, suggestive of a hybrid mode. Andrew Cowan's *Crustaceans* (2000) is another good example. The crustaceans in this novel are modern men, hidden in their shells and unable to make emotional contact with others. This is as bleak a novel of its type as one could imagine, a raw demonstration of futile love by a father – the novel's narrator, Paul – addressed to his dead son, Euan. The action of the novel's present occurs on a single day, which would have been Euan's sixth birthday, had he not died on the beach in a tragic accident the previous summer.

The inversion of the seaside stereotype – the scene now of familial tragedy, not the setting of a childhood idyll – involves also the disruption of routine patterns of thought. At one telling moment, Paul recalls his thoughts just after Euan was born (in his imagined

41

address to the boy at the age of six): 'my thoughts ran to the seashore in summer, absurdly, too hastily, for I knew the names of nothing we might find there, but already we were gathering shells, casting stones at the waves, raiding rockpools for crabs. Crustaceans. I knew that word at least, and I helped you pronounce it' (pp. 17–18). The true sense of imprisonment, here, is conveyed by the instantaneousness of the association, the desire to introduce the boy to the seaside, linked here, and throughout the novel, with emotional dysfunction. Paul's own boyhood memories of seaside holidays with his aunt are characterized by the absence of his father, aloof and distanced following the death of Paul's mother (p. 43). The seaside becomes an emblem of the source of paternal pain, usually perpetuated by rote, but which is here a burden located with Paul's generation: it is Paul, bereft of both father and son, who is the symbolic final repository of this burden, and the routine that produced it.

Perhaps the best of the seaside novels from this period is Chris Paling's *Deserters* (1996), another novel that trades on seaside stereotypes gone stale. Set mostly in Brighton, and with obvious echoes of Greene, Paling's novel anatomizes lives without pattern or structure, and is underpinned by an investigation of personal responsibility. It is centred on the career of Cliffie, the novel's bisexual, and unstable narrator, who enjoys his first settled domestic relationship with a backstreet café manager, Barry. An army deserter, Cliffie had originally planned to rob Barry, but is pulled up short, in his alcoholic haze, by a powerful moment of self-awareness: 'I caught a glimpse of myself leaning towards him in the bar mirror. It was so ludicrous and disconnected an image I almost shouted to him to watch his pockets because someone was trying to pick them. When I saw it was me I stopped and stared at myself; . . . I saw . . . someone who had good enough looks once but had all but destroyed them with booze and the needle. I saw a black leather jacket hanging on a wasted frame' (p. 8). This is a disturbing novel of lives destroyed by desertion, in the sense of the denial of responsibility to others. Cliffie's psyche is fractured by a buried memory from childhood, and the sexual violence he associates with a 'brown room'. For the character May, later redeemed by motherhood and life in a commune, her earlier insanity stems from a miscarriage, real or imagined. At one point, her madness infects Cliffie, when, responding to her insistence that a child is crying, he hears 'the plaintive cry of a child screaming against the wind' (p. 38). Like the promiscuous barroom scene in which Cliffie picks up Barry, the echo of May's sorrow in the sea air is an instance of inverted seaside experience – a child's scream, not the sound of beach games – to crystallize the essence of lives that have gone awry.

Paling takes the capacity of the seaside novel to distil the elements of social anomie to an extreme in *A Town by the Sea* (2005). This highly self-reflexive book is a parable, comprised of mini-parables, written in the form of an existentialist nightmare. The book's narrator, nameless for much of the book, is treated with brutality and incomprehension by the townsfolk when he appears on the beach and enters their town. The eventual discovery of his name – Marcelino Merida – and that he was a volunteer for the nationalist force in the Spanish Civil War before absconding, does not lend any sustained contextual meaning to the novel. Rather, it reveals continuity with the 'type' of narrator established in Cliffie in *Deserters*, who deserts rather than fight in the Falklands campaign, and whose life is crossed by the absence of a mother. Marcelino's discovery that his mother had died while he was fighting the war is what finally disconnects him from his social fabric, and which turns him, like Cliffie, into a drifter who is both target, and sometime perpetrator, of random acts of violence. In its brutal simplicity, *A Town by the Sea* exposes the skeleton of the seaside novel more usually fleshed out in the mode of realism: it is, in effect, a deconstruction of the genre.

A more central example is Graham Swift's *Last Orders* (1996), with its obvious echo of those lines from *The Waste Land*: 'On Margate Sands / I can connect / Nothing with nothing.' The allusion to Eliot's poem, that great literary statement mourning Western society's loss of faith in institutionalized belief, signals that Swift's novel makes the process of mourning revelatory of a broader spiritual crisis. It is the idea of the shabby seaside that punctures the solemnity of the symbolic journey of the mourners to Margate, to scatter the ashes of Jack Dodd in the sea.[18]

Swift's novel exemplifies the crisis of identity that dominates many varieties of the contemporary novel, where the available institutions highlight rather then ameliorate the sense of human fragility. In the British tradition, the seaside novel distils exactly this angst; but, paradoxically, its elegiac form, generated through the exposure of insubstantial social structures, has produced a new form of aesthetic consolation. At the end of *Last Orders*, the valedictory ritual marks not just the end of Jack Dodds, but also the symbolic termination of the friends who honour him, and who are of his generation. Yet Swift conjures a form of secular redemption through the communal operation of collective memory, and in this connection the seaside, as a focus for the characters' pilgrimage, is more than background: it is the social embodiment of this communal collective memory. This goes beyond the Jungian association of the sea with the collective unconscious. It identifies, rather, a particular phase of social history.

Understanding the place of the seaside in British cultural life depends upon a recognition of the 'deep cultural roots which the seaside had struck in popular consciousness, especially and tellingly in relation to children, by the early twentieth century'; by the late twentieth century, the British seaside 'maintained its power as a cultural referent', and did so partly by 'beginning to market itself in post-modern, ironic ways, inviting visitors to make jokes about seaside kitsch'. This ironic dimension has been an integral part of seaside experience for many generations, even if latterly it contributes to 'a distinctive experience which is also sold as part of the heritage tourist boom'.[19]

The prominence of the idea of the seaside holiday in children's literature is both a reflection of and possibly an explanation for the enduring power of the seaside in adult consciousness. Yet this 'innocent and timeless vision of the seaside' was partly 'embroidered' by 'the postwar generation ... from its own memories of childhood holidays'. Part of the progression to adulthood in British society is then explained by the recognition of how sanitized an idea this is, how seaside life in reality is characterized by such things as the economic hardship of seasonal work; sexual predation (and freedom);

the tawdry underbelly of variety entertainment; and the criminality that thrives where employment is unregulated.[20]

This recognition is more complex than it appears, more than the scales of childhood innocence falling from our eyes: after all, parents continue to take their children to the seaside in full consciousness of the seediness beneath the veneer. This is not simply because early child literacy and socialization in Britain is dominated by the association of 'seaside' and 'holiday' – that is true, but what makes the seaside especially compelling is its adult appeal. Partly this has to do with the elemental qualities of the sea and the coast, which make the location an accessible dramatic contrast with most working lives; yet the more interesting aspect of the appeal comes from its unique status as a space of extremes. In an extraordinarily simple psychological equation, a space literally 'on the edge', and away from the authoritarian strictures of routine, gives license to 'the spirit of carnival': here, 'where land and sea meet, the pleasure principle is given freer rein, the certainties of authority are diluted, and the usual constraints on behaviour are suspended.'[21]

This is not simply to dignify the presiding spirit of the seaside holiday camp, where childhood and adult pleasures can coexist, where parents can enjoy evening entertainment when their happy and exhausted offspring have fallen asleep. The appeal of the seaside as a liminal space has a more significant social aspect to it. The carnival spirit is one that admits social contradiction – the possibility of being ripped off at the funfair – as the necessary condition of a space of extremes. The seaside, that is to say, reveals manifestations of societal conflict and inequality that are either absent from middlebrow experience, or parcelled up in safe packages held at one remove.

Traditionally, the British seaside holiday was a great social leveller, bringing working- and middle-class families together, or at least in some kind of uncustomary proximity. As that old class divide has dissolved, however, seaside experience has acquired a different significance. The disappearance of the old working class, the expansion of the middle class, and the emergence of an amorphous underclass, have changed that dynamic. The centrality of the seaside holiday in British culture has also been shaken by the popularity of overseas holidays.

Yet the mythology of the seaside remains pervasive, as a presumed key experience of childhood; and the seaside stages a new social interaction – between that expanding middle class, and that wing of the underclass engaged in migrant and seasonal work. For the middlebrow family, seaside experience brings them closer to social paradox and contradiction than they usually get, and at a time when they are attuned to the idea of enjoyment. The seaside holiday, then, produces the flicker of a utopian effect; and the seaside novel reproduces something of this effect, vicariously, for its readers.

The novelists I have been discussing are attuned to ways in which seaside experience reveals key instances of social connection and social paradox; and it is clear that there has been an intensification of this propensity to be observed from the last quarter of the twentieth century. The British seaside resort appeared 'to pass into a time-warp' as a consequence of social and economic changes in the 1970s and 1980s, not least of which was the increasing availability and affordability of package holidays abroad.[22]

The economic decline of the British seaside since the 1980s is irrefutable, if sometimes overstated; it is, moreover, an important barometer of social change. John K. Walton links 'the problems of the more down-market resorts at the century's end' with 'the widening gulf in living standards between the better-off and the poor which had marked the social polarization of the Thatcher years and continued through the 1990s.'[23] Seaside decrepitude in the 1990s then takes on the hue of the new social divisions that obtain in 'post-class' Britain.

My broad argument is that the seaside novel of the 1990s distils the essence of social relations post-Thatcher, and does so by revitalizing the prosaic descriptiveness of provincial realism with the reflective tones of confessional narrative; and another novel that illustrates this combination clearly is *Trespass* (1998), by D. J. Taylor. Taylor uses a run-down hotel on the Suffolk coast as the setting that encapsulates his concerns. Holed up in this 'seaside hotel out of season', the kind of place where 'all the jetsam of English society comes to rest' (p. 19), narrator George Chell lives 'a vagrant existence' in the mid-1990s, living off investments (pp. 17–18). He has been aimless since the collapse of his uncle's business empire, Chell Holdings, six years previously. After an undistinguished start in life, he had become his uncle Ted's right-hand man, with him at his death, a broken man, disgraced by fraudulent trading, and making the revelation that we have been expecting all along: that he is really George's father (p. 306). Taylor's debt to Victorian and Edwardian fiction is clear, and quite self-conscious: this is social realism addressed to the condition of England, and in particular to the Thatcherite City of insider dealing and the fraudulent misuse of funds.

A publisher puts George in touch with a freelance writer, the dour Frances, who might ghost the (ill-fated) book he is planning to write about his uncle's life, and she comes to stay at his hotel, The Caradon, to conduct some interviews. An essential point of the book, and the basis for its credentials as a seaside novel, is that this Suffolk outpost, from where the revelations of the City of the 1980s are made – both through the interview transcripts, and George's retrospective narrative – is intimately connected with both the corruption and the confusion of that world. This is made clear when George discovers that the hotel's owner, the decidedly odd Mr Archer, was one of those investors who lost money at the collapse of Chell Holdings, and is probably the author of the hate mail George has been receiving at the hotel. At the end of her stay, Frances rails at George apropos of his habit of speculating about Mr Archer: 'Why don't you leave Archer alone? I mean, interfering in his life, cooking up all those little fantasies about him. It's just a kind of trespassing, when you think about it. Feeding off someone else's world' (p. 288). This simultaneously explains, and fudges, Taylor's choice of title: the defrauding of the small investor like Archer is paralleled by this new kind of trespassing on his life; yet speculation about the personal life is plainly the business of the novelist, an impulse that might well seem anathema to the brittle and unimaginative Frances. Archer is revealed as a lonely – and unexpectedly complicated – man, with a hopeless passion for one of his employees, and an altruistic and socially responsible impulse towards another, prone to petty theft. He is, that is to say, embroiled in his own messy microcosm of social contingency.

The same indeterminacy governs the novel's depiction of the era of 'conspicuous consumption' (p. 199). George has one telling memory of his uncle, distributing money from a wad of notes, in a vulgar charitable gesture that evokes a stereotype of the 1980s (made popular by the comedian Harry Enfield's creation, 'loadsamoney') (p. 314); but equally resonant is the sense that he was unaware of his misdeeds, that he acted in the spirit of an entrepreneurial age, insufficiently regulated (p. 311). Finally, this is not just a satirical novel about the City in the Thatcher era, but also a novel driven by the introspective impulses that reflect this era. George, the drifter in a seaside town, is simultaneously a rootless object of pity and a parasite: the novel ends with his vague sexual speculation about Brenda, the object of the late Archer's passion (p. 336). Again, the seaside is that place in which underlying social relations (and contradictions) are revealed.

The way in which the novel's realism is overlaid by introspection distinguishes it as a recognizable seaside novel. Paul Binding accounts for this blend with reference to 'the famous quarrel between Henry James and H. G. Wells', assuming, in this reworking of *Tono-Bungay*, that Taylor would 'take Wells's part'. Yet Taylor, 'at his own showing, would be mistaken', concludes Binding, since the strongest elements of *Trespass* come 'from the Jamesian within . . . not the Wellsian without'.[24] It may be the peculiar blend of these elements, however, that gives this, and the other seaside novels considered here, their power.

1996 seems to have been a particularly rich year for this type of seaside novel, seeing publication of Peter Benson's *The Shape of Clouds* and Paul Sayer's *The God Child*, as well as the key novels by Graham Swift and Chris Paling discussed above. Blanchard's *Wilson's Island* (1997) and Taylor's *Trespass* (1998) follow close behind. There can be little doubt that the end of the prolonged period of Conservative rule, the Thatcher-Major era, which saw many dramatic changes in British social relations – which were, in many cases, the manifestation of longer-term changes – provoked or inspired this kind of treatment. In the hands of these novelists, the seaside novel supplied a shorthand way of evoking those social relations that seemed to have been overlaid or by-passed in the age of the entrepreneur, and the advent of the so-called 'classless' society. It is also worth remarking that, although these novels seem to have internalized a form of social breakdown, they also comment upon it by concentrating, and so resuscitating, the essential ingredients of provincial realism. This under-recognized response to Thatcherism is also a vital (and underrated) bridge with tradition in the development of the English novel.

It is important to recognize that there is a longer tradition here, being honed for a specific context. Norman Levine's *From a Seaside Town* (1970), a novel with something of a cult following, demonstrates the broader connotations of rootlessness that are associated with the seaside novel. Levine's is a strange, plotless novel, narrated from the perspective of Joseph Grand, a Jewish Canadian whose identity bespeaks the uncertain quest for authentic artistic expression, under the sign of postwar migrancy. The elements of Grand's rootlessness seem to be aptly concentrated in a 'decaying seaside town in the south of England' (p. 30), revealing the longer-term economic and cultural collapse that suggested itself to novelists of the twentieth century.

In a still longer literary-historical perspective, the seaside novel is a genre one might point to to illustrate the shift from the confident novelistic portrayal of society, epitomized in the modes of omniscient narrative associated with nineteenth-century fiction, to a new convention of insularity and social breakdown, captured in the narrative forms of a hybridized provincial realism, and epitomized in the seaside novel of the 1990s. My insistence on the presence of this kind of convention should not detract from the variety and invention of the novel in Britain into the twenty-first century; but it does highlight the inadequacy of our critical models when a convention that looms so large should be absent from our critical surveys. This is a vital form of post-consensus fiction in itself, bearing few of the radical formal elements commonly associated with the most praised novels of the period. The question that must be asked is whether or not the neglect of such novels is, as I tend to think, a sign of critical prejudice. Here is a genre that exposes the simplicity of some post-consensus constructions in two ways: by demonstrating that telling responses to Thatcher were not always formally radical; and by revealing the longer historical undertow of those responses, with regard to formal expression as well as political change.

While I was writing this chapter, two novels by prominent British novelists were published, in which the seaside figures prominently: Ian McEwan's *On Chesil Beach* and Graham Swift's *Tomorrow* (both 2007). This suggests two things: first, that the preoccupations of contemporary provincial realism may well infiltrate mainstream literary culture in demonstrable ways; and second, that a new focus on the domestic may be a consequence of the increasing prominence given to portrayals of insularity and anomie in British fiction.

McEwan's novella, *On Chesil Beach* (2007), uses the idea of the seaside as a liminal space to embed, symbolically, its central premise: that one failed wedding night in 1962 can be taken as emblematic of the dividing line between the sexual liberation of the 1960s and the repression that preceded it. More particularly, Chesil Beach, that long stretch of pebbles that separates the English Channel from the Fleet Lagoon, is made to symbolize this epochal change. As the scene of confrontation on the wedding night, after the disastrous sexual encounter of newlyweds Edward and Florence, the beach – immensely difficult to walk on, like all pebble beaches – embodies their separation and failure to communicate. Despite the novella's historical ambition, to portray in miniature a generational shift in social mores, it is that focus on failed domestic experience that makes it so much of its time.

In Swift's *Tomorrow*, seaside experience frames the existence of the nuclear family unit that is Swift's focus: a romantic interlude on Brighton beach inaugurates the relationship of Paula and Mike; while a family memory of the near-drowning of their children, the twins Nick and Kate, while on holiday in Cornwall, underscores the fragility of this domesticity. Saved by their father on that occasion, the twins, now sixteen, are to hear a revelation on the 'tomorrow' the novel anticipates: they will discover that they were conceived through IVF, with sperm from an anonymous donor. This will deprive them of the biological father they thought they had, and so demolish the basis of the family unit that has sustained them.

Partly, this is a novel about the social impact of technology, in the spirit of Ishiguro's *Never Let Me Go* (2005); yet its focus is narrowly domestic. Both McEwan's novella, and Swift's novel, in their different ways, contribute to a new domestic fiction. The new emphasis on domesticity – prefigured, notably, in McEwan's *Saturday* (2005) – implies either a distinct shrinking of possibilities for the novel, or a specific form of response to the new processes of globalization. The tradition of the seaside novel must be seen as an important progenitor of this intriguing new phase of creativity.

2

The Novel and Cultural Life in Britain

Artistic endeavour in Britain is now dominated by the culture of prizes and awards; and for those involved in the promotion of art, the media controversy that accompanies the prize-giving process is always to be welcomed. As media exposure inevitably – and exponentially – increases the cultural capital of a painter or a writer, the old adage is repeatedly confirmed: there is no such thing as bad publicity.

In considering the question 'what is a work of art?', apropos of the furore caused annually in the tabloid press by the award of the Turner Prize, John Carey establishes the provisional suggestion that 'anything' can be art provided that 'someone thinks of it as a work of art'. While this might silence the elitism implicit in the routine ranting against BritArt, it also reveals why 'the art-world has lost its credibility'. The iconoclasm of contemporary art begets an egalitarianism which undermines its fiscal value: modern thought dissolves that 'separate category of things called works of art . . . which are intrinsically more valuable than things which are not works of art', thus making a nonsense of such works as 'Tracey Emin's £150,000 unmade bed'.[1] Yet this may be to overlook the conceptual and spatial claims implicit in contemporary art. But there is also a sensationalist aspect to the public presentation of conceptual art, which means that reputation depends on being the *first* to unveil, as art, an arrangement of bricks, or an unmade bed, or a creature preserved in formaldehyde. Of course, it is not just a question of being the first: it is also a question of being in a favourable situation to be *presented* as an original, worthy of attention. Timing is crucial.

This last point – essentially about the interrelationship of power and artistic fashion – is aptly illustrated for me by a memory from 1983 at my sister's degree show at Bath College of Art. While my sister Alison and most of the other students had each been allocated a favourable studio space, whitewashed and cleared for the degree show, and suited to more conventional offerings (canvases, sculptures, the occasional installation), there was one student who was not so fortunate. For reasons of health and safety, his show was confined to the nearby shed where he had practised his art for three years, and where few of the parents and siblings of the class of '83 dared to venture; for his show, if you could fight through the clouds of flies to discover, was on the theme of decomposition and preservation. It featured animal parts and carcases, some rotting, some inexpertly preserved in chemical solution. I have often wondered what became of this unsung innovator, a pariah in his artistic community, who graduated three years before Damien Hirst went to art college.

It is quite possible, of course, that the student of decomposition and preservation was not unique: perhaps there were similar undergraduate stunts at degree shows up and down the country in the early 1980s, and I need have no fear that the individual concerned must have been sent mad by the vicissitudes of the art world. However, the example does demonstrate some of the contradictions implicit in that wing of contemporary art designed to shock by virtue of its notional 'originality'. The Turner Prize, which was first awarded in 1984, brings to our attention the paradox of art in the marketplace, where originality may be a construction, and where reputation may be engineered by interests that have no aesthetic rationale or investment. We should remember that this prize, 'conceived as an equivalent of the Booker Prize', also 'reflected something of the entrepreneurial spirit of "Thatcher's Britain"'.[2]

In less sensational ways, literary prize culture is also mired in the paradox of the marketplace, and the contradictions that accompany the entrepreneurial spirit that has been abroad in Britain, from the 1980s onwards. A writer's fortune can be transformed by a prize or a nomination, as the recent impact of television's Richard and Judy's Book Club, with its associated Best Read of the Year Award has demonstrated.[3] Over a longer period, however – now nearly forty years – it is the Man Booker Prize that has been the dominant influence, and the institution that is usually held to have breathed the lifeblood back into British literary culture.

The importance of the Booker Prize to the novel in Britain – and, indeed, to the health of the novel in English more widely – has become an established fact of literary history. In the first edition of *The Modern British Novel* Malcolm Bradbury argued that the Booker had succeeded in 'encouraging publishers to support the serious novel at a time when there was a belief that its audience was dying, and of making good fiction a matter of public interest and debate'. He acknowledged those critics who felt the Booker had blurred the line between commerce and art, and those who felt it encouraged 'the writing of a mannerist prize-oriented fiction'. Yet he concluded that the Booker shortlists comprise 'a useful, illuminating chart of good fiction published from Britain from the turn of the Seventies onward.'[4] I think this claim is irrefutable – it will be tested later in this chapter, where I discuss some past winners – but the claim does tend to gloss over the ways in which the prize might have played a role in *constructing* our concept of serious fiction. It is also worth wondering if we have become accustomed to overestimating the role of the Booker.

Richard Todd's groundbreaking assessment of the Booker Prize and its impact on the novel in Britain is very much in tune with Bradbury: for Todd, the Booker's role in reinvigorating the novel weighs more heavily in the balance than do his worries about commodification. However, he also reminds us that the renaissance in British publishing from the 1980s merely returns us to the position of the late 1930s, before the paper shortages of the 1940s, since a comparable number of serious literary fiction titles had been published in 1939 as in 1980.[5]

The accepted role of the Booker must be viewed as an aspect of the literary critical myth of renaissance discussed in the previous chapter. The account is partially true, yet it serves to compound the distortions that result from the detection of a clear period break. If the Booker Prize has contributed to the revitalization of the fiction industry in Britain, this does not necessarily mean that the British novel in the 1960s and 1970s was an impoverished form, even if it was, temporarily, an endangered one. And if the Booker has helped to encourage a new variety, in style and subject matter, and a consequent greater choice for readers, it has merely assisted a process of democratization that was certainly already underway. The dominance of the mode of provincial realism, for instance, was already being shaken up.

It may be true that we are in a new phase of literary professionalism, and a new phase of literary commercialism, a phase that generates new forms of self-consciousness, for readers as well as writers. And it may be that literary prize shortlists are often taken as credible 'consumer guides', with prizes such as the Whitbread and the Orange contributing to this merging of commerce and evaluation. Yet this has led to the questionable idea that, in chasing prizes, writers transform their art for the marketplace; and the Booker has been seen as particularly culpable in this connection.

Academics and journalists have both pondered the new kind of self-conscious performance implicit in 'the idea that a certain kind of novelist may actually deliberately set out to write a "generic" Booker winner'.[6] I find this suggestion generally implausible (with the exception of the example discussed below: Ian McEwan's *Amsterdam*). Even so, the Booker 'shortlistees' have exerted an influence on the literary culture in the same way that prominent novels in earlier eras had done – that is, by gradually fashioning public taste (and so concentrating the minds of publishers); and by influencing the work of other writers, by giving them exempla to feed on and react to. This is not to reinforce the idea that a 'generic' Booker winner can be planned with a slide-rule, but rather to say that the Booker has a central role in the focusing of that artistic innovation that was previously more dissipated and harder to track.

In a more abstract sense, however, it is the idea of serious fiction that is validated in the new culture of the literary prize. The serious fiction that is now constructed through the commodification of the artefact in our literary prize culture is hard to define, but Clive Bloom hits on a key aspect of it when he observes that 'new serious novels' are 'usually the standard bearers of a long tradition of humanist moral enquiry'. The business of prize selection and giving validates this tradition of 'the literary canon as an unbroken moral project and the serious novel at its centre'. Bloom astutely observes that where for Matthew Arnold in the nineteenth century, or for the Leavises in the twentieth, literary culture was a civilizing force to oppose the effects of industry and commerce – despite the paradox that 'only in the marketplace could good taste be properly validated' – literary culture is now clearly wedded to commerce, with the literary prize as 'the most overt form of that validating procedure'. The process of reconciling 'good taste and commercial success' in the awarding of literary prizes produces something distinctive, a form of ' "serious" commercial fiction aimed at middle-to highbrow readers', which is 'a literary genre' in its own right.

The problem is compounded for critics like Bloom by the opaque manner of judging, or rather, the presumed unselfconsciousness of literary prize judges – 'the masons of serious literature' – because they form a professional elite prosecuting its own interests, and without sufficient self-examination. Bloom acknowledges the function of the Booker Prize in bringing authors and novels 'to the attention of a wider public'. Yet he is much exercised by the lack of objectivity in the judging process: prize judges, like book reviewers, can do no more than try to give their prejudices, their gut reactions some form of authoritative expression. As Booker judges are often also novelists and critics, the idea of serious fiction in that long tradition of humanist moral enquiry is unlikely to be shaken.[7]

That there is a long tradition casts doubt, of course, on the notion that prize culture has had a transformative effect. But it is the pejorative sense in which 'humanist moral enquiry' is intended that exposes the real critical issue, here. Academic critics who agree with this censure will restrict themselves to a condemnatory stance, driven to snipe at contemporary literary culture as a dubious manifestation of late capitalism (which would be a travesty). The challenge is then to conceive of an acceptable form of critical enquiry that might facilitate appreciation of the contemporary novel, in spite of its commercial taint.

A pragmatic way of looking at the problem of judgement in the awarding of a prize is to see the *difficulty* of making a judgement, and the conflict between subjectivity, and that notional aspiration of objectivity, as being unavoidable. When judges disagree, the resulting compromise might still seem to consolidate a traditional notion of value; but only after the difficulty of judging has been exposed. And when conflicts arise, and spill out into the media, a healthy debate can follow. Bloom discusses one famous spat, when Nicholas Mosley resigned from the 1991 panel of judges after none of his preferred novels made the shortlist. A protracted debate about 'the novel of ideas' in the British press ensued. Bloom suggests that it may be to the credit of the Booker to have instigated 'a more public discussion' on this topic, though he feels the attendant 'issues remain obtuse and confusing'.[8] It seems to me, however, that it would be inconceivable to imagine a debate about literary form taking place in the national press now without the media prominence of the Booker Prize. Yet there is also continuity in this, with the media circus of the literary prize generating those debates that were more commonplace in the quality press in earlier eras.

This does not, however, pin down the ways in which business interests infiltrate art through prize culture, under the sign of entre-preneurship, which is surely a new departure. As James English has pointed out, it is what follows from this infiltration that is both hard to dismiss and to define. This is the other form of economics – the '*cultural* economics of prizes and awards' – or, what English terms 'the economics of cultural prestige'. This form of economics, which is not 'based on money', but which 'cannot be understood apart from the money economy', is elusive of interpretation. It requires that we extend our understanding of economics in relation to artistic production 'to include systems of non-monetary, cultural, and symbolic transaction'.

In his introduction, English acknowledges a positive dimension to prize culture that is difficult to keep in view in any critique. Aside from the 'calculation and dealmaking', the 'marketing strategy and self-promotion', we ought also to reckon with the 'generosity, celebration, love, play, community' that are part and parcel of the cultural prize-giving process. Sensibly, English understands that 'every type of capital everywhere is "impure"'; this means that it behoves 'every holder of capital' to put 'his or her capital to work in an effort to defend or modify the ratios of that impurity'.[9] This moral exhortation must also apply to professional critics, journalistic or academic, as much as it does to novelists and prize sponsors. It might also invoke the responsibility of readers; but it may be through the very imperfections and contradictions of the Booker that this kind of self-consciousness is encouraged. It may also be that the 'media circus' aspect of prize culture is now an accepted part of it. The ambivalence that surrounds prizes is evident to all: critics, readers, novelists are all involved in a self-conscious pact, in which something of value is wilfully derived, even while the contradictions are fully apparent.

All of this points to economic changes affecting cultural production, but without demonstrating the occurrence of a sea-change in the form of the novel. For subscribers to the post-consensus narrative, however, the fact that the Booker began to become a media event in the Thatcher era is telling. Originally, the winning title had been announced prior to the award ceremony, but from 1979, the result was withheld until the moment of presentation. This significant change generated the suspense, speculation and media attention that we have come to associate with the Booker. 1979 was also the year in which a more formalized Management Committee membership was introduced.[10] The mood of entrepreneurship associated with the 1980s was certainly reflected in the fortunes of the Booker, the presentation of which was televised live between 1981 and 2005.[11]

An example may help to focus the degree to which the Booker has encouraged a new type of novel. The Booker winner that most obviously engages with the literary consequences of Thatcherism, with the impact on the writer's vocation of that form of individualism associated with entrepreneurial self-promotion, is Ian McEwan's *Amsterdam* (1998). By common consent, *Amsterdam* is not McEwan's best book; indeed, it is widely held to be an inferior – even an undeserving – Booker winner. It is, however, the one winner that seems to me pointedly written *for* the Booker, not as a 'generic' winner based on previous successes, but as a consummately realized work within strict limits.

On those occasions when a writer wins a literary prize for a book that does not showcase his or her best work, work that has gone unrewarded in the past, it is invariably suggested that the judges have sought to right previous wrongs, and have made an award for past work, rather than for the book in question. Certainly, McEwan had previously been shortlisted for the Booker, in 1981, for *The Comfort of Strangers*, and again in 1992, for *Black Dogs*. Yet his much-admired *Enduring Love* had failed to reach the shortlist in 1997 (as had his excellent novel *The Child in Time* a decade earlier). It is hard to resist the suspicion that McEwan, perhaps sensing that his time had come, produced *Amsterdam* rapidly for the 1998 Prize. Given the novella's theme of professional competitiveness, we might also wonder if McEwan sought to benefit from the cultural capital generated by his growing reputation in an archly self-conscious gesture: was *Amsterdam* a form of 'spoiler' designed to defeat the ambitions of other contenders?[12]

It is possible to make too much of this, since any novelist put forward for the Booker hopes to win, and to 'spoil' the ambitions of the other contenders. Yet there are grounds for thinking that *Amsterdam* betrays a good deal of self-reflexiveness in its satire. To begin with, the idea of a 'spoiler' is central to McEwan's concerns, signalling that contemporary form of self-contained professionalism that lacks an ethical dimension. The two principal characters, news-paper editor Vernon Halliday and composer Clive Linley, both encounter an ethical dilemma that reveals how morality has been displaced by self-interest in the world of the contemporary professional.

This is a straightforward satire of a new form of professionalism that is patently invulnerable to ethical demands or to questions of social responsibility; and it is the context for this satire that makes it significant and interesting. In *Amsterdam*, McEwan addresses, obliquely, the uncomfortable paradox that the Thatcher-Major era may have generated an apparent renaissance in English fiction (in the

59

fashionable view), even though writers were largely hostile to the political ethos associated with Thatcherism. Of course, this may simply suggest that the serious literary response to politics feeds on moral outrage; yet the awkward fact remains that, after seventeen years of Conservative government, some of the Tories' fiercest critics had become the beneficiaries of the very policies they had denounced. There are always accidents of circumstance – a career must be built, regardless of who is in power – but McEwan is interested in the point where ideology infiltrates the professional consciousness.

It seems to me clear that the plight of the writer, which is McEwan's plight, too, is implicated in *Amsterdam*'s satirical portrait of left-intellectual achievement after 1979. That term 'spoiler' is crucial, here. It is used in two key instances: first, when Vernon Halliday's front-page photograph of the foreign secretary in drag is exposed before the television cameras before it is published, so that his coup, his front page 'classic which would one day be taught in journalism school', is 'spoiled' (pp. 116, 124). The second occurrence is at the end, when Halliday, realizing that Linley has killed him in an act of mutual, enforced euthanasia, acknowledges 'reverentially' this 'spoiler' (p. 173).

The reverence of the act of spoiling underscores the novella's central satirical thrust: that we live in an era when professional standards are established in a moral vacuum; and this becomes especially troubling if we read the novella as a self-conscious deliberation about literary prize culture. For if *Amsterdam* is itself a 'spoiler', written hastily to maximize McEwan's cultural capital and sweep the 1998 Booker, we are surely invited to see it as up to its neck in the mire of self-regarding professionalism that it also satirizes. Pursuing this line, one reviewer perceived 'a satisfying irony in knowing that this is exactly the kind of book that the society McEwan satirizes would pick as the best book of the year'.[13]

The irony is *knowing*, however, and that makes it much more unsettling, and the novella far less simplistic, than is often assumed. The Booker Prize is a cultural product of the era that *Amsterdam* satirizes, so the novella is an implicit commentary, for the 1998 Booker judges, on the culture they would play their part in evaluating and supporting. The literary merit of the novella is then partly determined by its status as a literary *event*, where the satire bleeds out into the world of literary culture. What is 'spoiled', finally, is any residual notion that literary culture is immune to political or ideological influence. In this respect, the neatness of the novella's plotting, which annoyed many reviewers, has a purpose. Although it is not an inappropriate feature of a finely turned novella, this is one of the ways in which McEwan implicates himself in the debate about professionalism. The book's patness, which is at odds with its satirical thrust, projects its debate about morality and professional standards outwards, inviting us to think more seriously about them; and it is this process of making the satire bleed outwards, to encompass the book as a literary event and a complicitous agent in the literary prize culture exemplified by the Booker, that gives it its resonance.

This also places the book squarely in that tradition of moral enquiry associated with serious fiction. McEwan's wry satire may demonstrate that the appreciation of contemporary literature is now inextricably bound up with the literary prize, and that the contradictions inherent in the project of evaluation are also necessarily part of the critic and reader's business. But this may be to add another layer of self-consciousness to our understanding of literary culture, rather than to undermine it, or to suggest it is radically new in other ways. Even so, if consumers of the Booker shortlist may be conscious of the compromises that lie behind it, it still has a determining influence on who is read now, and on the type of novel that will be read in future. It is here that academic critics have found particular cause for concern.

Graham Huggan puts his discussion of the Booker Prize into the context of 'a global cultural economy controlled by huge multinational companies' overseeing 'the corporate sponsorship of the arts'. This may imply a greater sense of design and influence than is really the case, since corporate arts sponsorship is more haphazard than is sometimes assumed. A 'fit' is always needed between the company profile and the particular event favoured with sponsorship money; but the driving motive is invariably good press by association, rather than the desire to control or direct particular artistic practices. (The role of multinational media companies in the fashioning of cultural outputs, where there is an issue of ownership, may be less benign.) The Booker Prize is a special case; the fact that it has been associated with the promotion of postcolonial writing reveals a particular commercial irony, since Booker plc, formerly the Booker McConnell company, has a colonial past. The company, Huggan points out, was 'initially formed in 1834 to provide distributional services on the sugar-estates of Demerara (now Guyana)', and 'achieved rapid prosperity under a harsh colonial regime'.[14] English considers this to be a form of 'cultural money-laundering' that enables arts sponsors – like Booker, in the company of 'other colonial agribusiness companies in the early postcolonial era' – to improve their public image.[15]

The prominence of Booker winners from former Commonwealth countries, and from Britain, concerned with imperial themes, has frequently been observed, begging the question of the extent to which we should celebrate Booker's role as 'a postcolonial literary patron'. Huggan considers the proposition that the Booker has broken down literary frontiers, with the effect of challenging British insularity and nostalgia about its Empire. Against that view, however, he pursues 'the possibility that prizes like the Booker might work to contain cultural (self-)critique by endorsing the commodification of a glamorized cultural difference'. This is a charge that must be seriously addressed, since it seeks to identify an aesthetic veneer that conceals a form of ideological bad faith, and an aesthetic that, in turn, fosters self-deception in a reader with any kind of investment, conscious or unconscious, in the hegemonic centre. It is a sophisticated instance of that form of academic analysis from which the naïve reader emerges as the ideological dupe of a disastrously compromised cultural form.

There is also the problem of a prize funded and administered in Britain, and centred very much on the British publishing industry. There are, Huggan observes, 'structural differences in conditions of literary production and consumption across the English-speaking world'; which suggests that, if the prize celebrates cultural pluralism as Todd claims, then, for Huggan, it is a '*British* cultural pluralism' that is endorsed.

With reference to Booker winners like J. G. Farrell's *The Siege of Krishnapur* (1973) and Paul Scott's *Staying On* (1977), Huggan acknowledges the self-mockery that accompanies the undermining of imperial achievement; yet he also discerns a form of nostalgia, especially in *Staying On*, that supports a fantasy of the Raj, an ideological construct of the past, and a reprehensible 'exoticization of (colonial) history'. The Booker's role in regard to 'such potentially retrograde cultural products' is then to '*legitimize* them, promoting them for a wider public'. Because several of the Booker winners 'belong to a recognized postcolonial canon', the prize participates in the processes of canonization, and does so by 'privileging ... a certain kind of highly aestheticized "political writing" under the sign of the postcolonial' with the 'ironic effect of shutting down, or at least deflecting public attention away from, more radically unorthodox alternatives.'[16]

In a sense, that charge is unanswerable. It raises, again, the phantasm of a post-humanist form of fiction in which conventional forms of moral enquiry are absent. At the same time, we might wonder whether or not postmodernist experimentation has already infiltrated the Booker shortlists sufficiently to make readers ponder the form and limits of fiction in ways they might not otherwise have done.[17] Perhaps the most damaging charge concerns that exoticization of colonial history, together with the notion that this is a form of writing the Booker positively encourages.

A brief note about Booker winners writing on postcolonial themes may, at least, help us pin down something about literary identity in this connection. A writer much vilified in postcolonial criticism is V. S. Naipaul, whose book *In A Free State* was the winner in 1971, and, as in much of his fiction, his own sense of marginal ethnicity lends a literary and historical framework to the piece, though the insecurity, here, is projected onto Europeans.

J. G. Farrell's *The Siege of Krishnapur* (1973) offers an ambivalent treatment of imperialism, since the condemnation of the British in India is slightly compromised by the narrative perspective, which is concentrated with the British. Yet this is inevitable in a novel that subjects the codes of the adventure narrative to ironic treatment, with great comic effect. The ambivalence is neatly explained, perhaps, in Farrell's remark about his own ethnicity: 'Being half Irish and half English . . . I'm able to look at the same thing from both sides – from that of the colonist and the colonized.'[18]

Paul Scott's *Staying On* (1977), a coda to his Raj Quartet, contains its own ironic commentary on the Quartet's epic treatment of the last five years of British India: here we see the pitiful efforts of a retired army couple, Tusker and Lucy Smalley, to assert themselves and 'stay on' in India after Independence. The death of Tusker is announced at the outset, and the novel then works back to this point in a temporal loop to create a poignant love story, concerning a couple by-passed by history. (As a Booker winner it is all the more affecting given that Scott was dying of cancer when he received the prize.)[19]

Gordimer's *The Conservationist* (joint winner in 1974) is a complex allegorical and prophetic novel about political change in South Africa, written at a time when apartheid was deeply entrenched: it takes its place in Gordimer's oeuvre, an evolving response to the iniquities of political oppression. Her countryman J. M. Coetzee's Booker winners, *Life and Times of Michael K* (1983) and *Disgrace* (1999), represent different stages in his career-long struggle to reconcile modernist expression, historical guilt, and a professional conviction about the necessary distinction between fiction and History.

In all of these cases, it is clear that the writer's subject is determined by ethnicity, deep commitment, career profile, or all of the above, so that it is quite proper to refuse the suggestion that these writers chose their subjects, and to argue that their subjects chose them. The decision of publishers to promote particular authors is less amenable to scrutiny; though the global resonance of these topics is self-evident. Another example is furnished by a more recent Booker winner, a book that is interesting in this discussion because it reveals a form of literary nostalgia that will doubtless annoy those critics who bemoan the conventional profile of the postcolonial Booker novel.

The tradition of Booker winners set in India continued in 2006 when the prize was awarded to Kiran Desai for *The Inheritance of Loss*. For Desai, there was a family tradition, too, acknowledged in her thanks to her mother, Anita Desai, who had been on the Booker shortlist on three occasions.[20] Although *The Inheritance of Loss* engages with contemporary questions – most notably, the forms of inequality consequent upon globalization – it might be seen to have a foot in the past.

The emotional centre of the book is the household in the north-eastern Himalayas in which Sai, an orphaned Indian teenager, grows up, living with her Anglophile grandfather, a retired judge. Sai's love for her tutor Gyan is soured when he joins an Indian-Nepalese insurgency. In a parallel narrative, the cook's son, Biju, experiences successive disappointments as an illegal alien in New York, before returning, stripped by the insurgents of all his belongings, to enjoy a moving reunion with his father, at Sai's grandfather's house, on the final page.

Thus, despite the theme of globalization, this is a familiar narrative of the legacy of imperialism, and the internal instability and political corruption that occurs in the post-colonial vacuum – and so similar, in these respects, to V. S. Naipaul's *A Bend in the River*, shortlisted for the Booker in 1979. Naipaul's novel was written in the shadow of Conrad, so it is pertinent to consider exactly what 'tradition' Desai is contributing to. Helpfully, Desai has two of her characters discuss Naipaul. This is where the character Lola reports that she is finding *A Bend in the River* an 'uphill task', and is contradicted by her sister Noni, who considers it 'one of the best books' she has ever read. Lola demurs:

> 'I think he's strange. Stuck in the past.... He has not progressed. Colonial neurosis, he's never freed himself from it. Quite a different thing now. In fact,' she said, 'chicken tikka masala has replaced fish and chips as the number one take-out dinner in Britain. It was just reported in the *Indian Express*.' (p. 46)

Desai's ironic picture of the banal trappings of globalization, seen here in that snippet of a syndicated article about take-away food, evidently undercuts the criticism made of Naipaul. The popularity of chicken tikka masala in Britain may be a manifestation of a new form of global culture, but clearly not the reversal that might shake someone from a state of 'colonial neurosis'. One damaging consequence of globalization in a popular-intellectual sense, which is implicitly observed here by Desai, is that ideas about postcolonialism become simplified, indistinct and portable, so that a discussion about Naipaul's treatment of Africa can be elided with a fanciful notion about the changing cultural relationship between Britain and India.

It is true, however, that *A Bend in the River*, like much of Naipaul's work, is partly concerned with the Indian diaspora, so the connection made by Desai's characters could be justified, if followed through: Naipaul's narrator, Salim, is an East African Muslim of Indian descent. Yet the focus is Africa: the novel, set in a central African state based on Zaire, is concerned with the relationship between dictatorship and the idea of African 'authenticity'. This investigation is conducted through the rule of the dictatorial president, the Big Man, who is modelled closely on Mobutu. The central tension in Naipaul's analysis is that between tribal tradition and the superimposition of the modern state, which emerges as a misplaced European export.

The inevitability and the ambivalence of European influence are caught in Salim's thoughts on first visiting London. He reflects on the 'old Europe' that 'had defeated the Arabs in Africa and controlled the interior of the continent', and which ruled his world as a child. The post-imperial 'new Europe' of his adulthood, he reflects, 'still fed us in a hundred ways with its language and sent us its increasingly wonderful goods, things which, in the bush of Africa, added year by year to our idea of who we were, gave us that idea of our modernity and development.' The experience of London is unsettling for Salim, revealing a continuity between the hard-working traders of Africa and the toil of London traders that he begins to see 'as instinct, pointless, serving only itself' (pp. 268–70).

This is, apparently, a revelation about the basis of European power, rooted in profit and exploitation; yet it also forms a bridge to Naipaul's inspiration in Conrad, articulated in his essay 'A New King for the Congo: Mobutu and the Nihilism in Africa', written in 1975. Here he cites Conrad's observation in the Congo in 1890 of people, acting as agents of imperialism, 'who were too simple for an outpost of progress', their position of power an accident of circumstance, 'unredeemed by an idea'. In the same location eighty-five years later, Naipaul finds history repeating itself:

> The people who come now – after the general flight – are like the people who came then. They offer goods, deals, technical skills, the same perishable civilization; they bring nothing else. They are not pioneers; they know they cannot stay.[21]

Where the essay discovers a depressing continuity of European opportunism between 1890 and 1975, the novel reveals, through Salim's dark revelation at the sight of London traders, how something of that opportunism has been appropriated by Africans. In the essay, there is a more disturbing reversal, when Naipaul suggests that Conrad's Kurtz, ensconced in Stanleyville (the Stanley Falls station in the Congo of 1890), was realized in the person of Pierre Mulele, who led a rebellion and established a reign of terror at Stanleyville after Independence in the 1960s:

> Seventy years later, at this bend in the river, something like Conrad's fantasy came to pass. But the man with 'the inconceivable mystery of a soul that knew no restraint, no faith, and no fear' was black, and not white; and he had been maddened not by contact with wilderness and primitivism, but with the civilization established by ... pioneers.[22]

For some, this may indeed seem a form of colonial neurosis. From Naipaul's perspective, however, the influence of Conrad serves to bring into focus either a postcolonial or neo-colonial point of interregnum. Indeed, in his essay on Conrad (1974), Naipaul is insistent on the unique contemporary relevance: 'Conrad's value to me is that he is someone who sixty to seventy years ago meditated on my world, a world I recognize today. I feel this about no other writer of the century.'[23] The familiar complaint in postcolonial criticism that Naipaul is retrogressive in his treatment of colonial issues may betray an impatience that is insensitive to the slow and sometimes degenerative march of history.

A Bend in the River develops the sense of postcolonial collapse in Africa that characterizes *In a Free State*, the title novella from Naipaul's Booker-winning collection (1971). Set in a newly independent African country, *In a Free State* focuses on the political turmoil that accompanies decolonization. The protagonists who suffer these effects, Bobby and Linda, are European; yet their experiences anticipate the effect of *A Bend in the River* in that they are marginal figures caught up in larger political events. Indeed, the novella traces a series of humiliations in which European characters are revealed as impotent, culminating in the scene where Bobby is brutally beaten by soldiers at a checkpoint, for no reason (pp. 232–3). To a degree, Bobby, an administrator with a proclivity for buying sexual favours from African men (unsuccessfully in the narrative present of the novella), symbolizes colonial power and exploitation on the wane; yet the predominant effect is to create a sense of Africa as a brooding threat to the outsider, rather than to offer any form of sustained political analysis. This aspect of Naipaul's African fiction – a key legacy from Conrad – gives rise to impatience from the perspective of postcolonial criticism. One cannot find in the novella, as Fawzia Mustafa points out, 'a deeper awareness of the political complexities and economic handicaps created by Africa's colonization'.[24] This is justified criticism; but it does not make the work any the less compelling, taken on its own terms. Such complaints, when they accumulate to produce an orthodox view, carry with them a normative impulse, effectively outlawing different emphases.

Where might one turn for a novel about colonization and ethnicity, untainted by association with the Booker? One such novel, an important book about black British experience, is S. I. Martin's *Incomparable World* (1996), acknowledged as 'one of the more influential novels of the 1990s'.[25] This historical novel, set in London in 1786–7, imagines the plight of those black Americans who settled in London after fighting on the British side in the American War of Independence. Despite the hardship of black existence, under threat from poverty, slavery and random violence, there is an insistence on a form of English affiliation, by necessity: in Brazil, for example, certain of the characters find themselves bound to white English sailors by 'a common tongue' (p. 194). This realization of a cultural bond of necessity is the historical root of a tradition of black British writing into which the novel inserts itself: Martin implicitly appeals to this tradition, for example, when he has the main protagonist Buckram meet both Olaudah Equiano and Ottobah Cugoano during the course of his adventures.[26]

Yet this is no tale of multicultural celebration: it is clear that Martin intends the struggles of his characters to survive in London to mirror a contemporary state of inequality. Early in the novel Buckram is 'seized by a delirious vision' of a future England transformed through 'African worship and celebration' to 'a greater, more wholesome dance of life'. Martin can only partially see himself as one of the 'imperial orphans in communion with a fractured past', by virtue of such cultural hybridity: Buckram's alternative future resonates more loudly, perhaps, where his future kinsfolk remain 'hovering by closed doors, waiting for scraps from the master's table' (p. 45). In conversation with Ottobah Cugoano, Martin has Olaudah Equiano assert that black people 'will become, if indeed we are not already, an ineradicable element of this nation's character' (p. 117). The novel's historical lens, however, lays stress on the predictability, and the continuity, of inequality: 'there would always be black people starving about the streets of London ... for two hundred years this had been their condition here. Would another two centuries bring any change?' (p. 210).

The epigraph from Ignatius Sancho – 'I am only a lodger – and hardly that' – stresses the precariousness of black British experience; yet it also gestures towards that marginal condition of migrancy from which counter-cultural currents can emerge. Self-consciously, Martin tries to claim this position for himself, though this does make the appeal to the historical tradition of black British writing decidedly ambivalent: it remains marginal, after two hundred years.

It is easy to see why this fine novel was so influential, not just as a vividly realized historical novel, but as a political rallying point for other writers.[27] Yet, at the same time, it may reveal much in common with those novels that have attracted disapproval by virtue of aestheticizing the ethnic experience on the margins of society.

One could not accuse Martin of cultivating a position of marginality self-consciously: it is impoverishment – and the continuity of impoverishment – that his novel associates with this margin, even while it establishes a moral vantage point. In this respect one might see a clear difference between the studied and commodified marginality that postcolonial critics have sometimes sought to expose in postcolonial Englishness, and the dignity through restrained anger that allows us to feel Martin to be at one with Buckram at the end of *Incomparable World*, 'ready to claim whatever present the heart of England holds for him' (p. 213).

At the same time, it is impossible to deny that there is a process of 'aestheticizing' the historical experience that the novel presents through vivid fictional episode. We should, perhaps, set aside the issue of language in this connection. The use of standard English diction is probably deliberate, given the novel's theme of a common language as the basis of a shared but problematic inheritance for blacks and whites. There is also the practical impossibility of conjuring the diction of eighteenth-century black American migrants in London. (It is plainly easier for a Sam Selvon, or a Norman Smith, to import contemporaneous authentic black speech into the English novel.)[28]

The aspect that could be seen as problematic, if one were so minded, is the convention that Martin adopts of the bawdy/salacious historical fiction. One five-page sequence (pp. 88–93) will suffice to make the point: here Buckram recounts his prison experiences, confined in a cell with nine other crazed men. They fight over their food 'like wild dogs', and their jailors throw a young girl in their cell now and again for sport – some are killed. Buckram explains that he was then forced to spend a year performing sexual acts with a series of prostitutes for a paying audience, before rebelling and being 'awarded one thousand and five hundred lashes'. The chapter then moves to a bar scene in which a man's throat is cut, and his blood spills into the drinkers' ale tankards.

Of course, in this there is a process of aestheticizing extreme sadism and violence, in that genre of vividly rendered historical debauchery, and putting it to the service of gripping narrative. It would be possible to argue that, in this, there is an attempt to generate a form of fascination that exoticizes both the historical experience and the black experience simultaneously, making it wholly 'other' to the middlebrow contemporary reader. The fascination in the adventure, one might argue, is facilitated through the aestheticizing/sanitizing of historical suffering, in a dynamic that undercuts the continuity that Martin's novel is otherwise at pains to stress. The objection is ludicrous, of course, because novelistic form always aestheticizes experience in order to fascinate or please the reader. The example is extreme, but it should make us wary of accepting the arguments about the aestheticizing of experience that are becoming routine in postcolonial critiques of novels like *Brick Lane* and *White Teeth*.

The simple point I am making is that it may be impossible to conceive of a viable form of narrative fiction that treats of marginalized experience without subjecting it to some form of exoticization or aestheticization or selectivity, or without bringing a moralizing frame, however implicitly, to that experience. These features, perhaps, help define the limits of contemporary fiction; but it is hard to see what the alternatives are.

To try and clinch the point, following the model of the previous chapter, I shall again consider that deeply unfashionable form of novel writing, apparently invulnerable to exoticization, which has not been popular with the Booker judges, but which continues to be written: English provincial realism. A rare success was Stanley Middleton, probably the least fashionable Booker winner, who shared the prize in 1974 with Nadine Gordimer. Two more contrasting writers it is hard to imagine: where Gordimer was chronicling the most pernicious period of apartheid for an international audience – and was doing so in the 1970s and 1980s with increasing invention – Middleton was ploughing the predictable furrow of provincial realism. Regional writers can, of course, choose more expansive modes; yet Middleton combines these aspects, to write regional fiction in the mode of provincial realism, and the final ingredient in this recipe for unfashionableness is Middleton's choice of subject matter: middle-class experience. Reading Middleton is like reading David Storey or Alan Sillitoe, but without the class edge.

Holiday, Middleton's fourteenth novel, and one of the seaside novels considered in chapter one, is representative of his art. The 'holiday' is that taken by 32-year-old Edwin Fisher, returning to the Lincolnshire seaside resort of his childhood summers, but finding no escape from his failing marriage. The novel concerns the efforts of his in-laws to effect a reconciliation between Fisher and his estranged wife, Meg, and his own efforts to come to terms with the past. There are two central issues: first, the tragedy of infant mortality that has overshadowed the marriage; and, second, Fisher's need to address the dominant influence his father has had over his life. The marriage is saved, the issue of paternal power wrestled with and seemingly resolved.

In summary this sounds distinctly unadventurous and not the stuff of prize-winning fiction; yet the understated or oblique methods Middleton deploys make this an affecting and unassuming novel, and one which is revealing about masculinity, since the style is well suited to an age in which male emotions were habitually concealed. However, I do not imagine for a moment that this is enough to convert teachers of postwar fiction to the Middleton camp in their droves. A novel about middle-class marital strife will seem irredeemably dull to most, I expect, even if there is persuasive use of style.

Is it reasonable, however, for us to dismiss so habitually a mode of novel writing that has remained a constant presence in the British novel? In the case of Middleton, it is the issue of class, I suspect, that makes him seem so unfashionable. Yet it may be that his oeuvre, from 1958 until the twenty-first century, charts the subtle ways in which being 'middle class' in Britain has shifted. Indeed, this is one of the most significant, yet most elusive, social changes in the postwar period, and Middleton may have established a unique position in the British novel since 1950 by virtue of having chronicled those changes. This surely makes his fiction highly significant, if only from a sociological point of view.

In a later novel, *Small Change* (2000), Middleton allow himself a dig at literary prize culture, and, one assumes, at the Booker in particular. This occurs when the retired schoolteacher, Frank Norman, recounts a review of a novel to explain his own phlegmatic approach to life. The novel in question concerned the tribulations of a farmer, and the concerns of his family, which the reviewer praises for its accuracy, while finding it dull. Norman cannot help feeling that the reviewer wanted sensation – murder, bestiality, child abuse, AIDS. The lack of sensation, however, is only one aspect of the bias against English provincial realism that Norman detects:

> I have a suspicion that if the writer had set the same dull stuff in the Dordogne and Tuscany or Rhodesia, Zimbabwe, if that's what they call it now, it would have been more acceptable, whereas I felt privileged to share or empathize with the not very out of the ordinary life of the sort of man I'll see next time I walk out of the village. (pp. 92–3)

Despite the political narrowness of the character revealed here, Middleton is able to demonstrate a cosmopolitan impulse. He shows that provincial realists can do metafiction, too, and makes an implicit plea for his own kind of fiction, and the value of encouraging readers to empathize with ordinary experience.

In *Sterner Stuff* (2005), Middleton's protagonist Frank Montgomery, a gifted portrait painter of traditional style, and the principal of a northern art college, is made to carry the argument about artistic worth. Montgomery is an excellent administrator, earmarked as a future pro vice-chancellor when his college is merged with a university; yet he finally decides to follow the advice of his late father, and to put his art first. This decision opens up the issue of national tradition and culture, as he has been commissioned to paint a portrait of the Queen. In all of this there is something overblown, insofar as it connects with the proven provincial realism of Middleton, deemed to be old-fashioned in precisely the way Montgomery knows his painting will soon be assessed. At the same time, there is a quiet plea for tradition, and for the enduring form of fiction exemplified by Middleton.

When he is interviewed for the job of principal, Montgomery is asked for his opinion about artistic prize culture (in an allusion to the Turner Prize), and for his view as to whether or not 'carcases, piles of books, a mould laid round an empty house, an unmade bed' qualify as works of art. Montgomery replies, first, that the composition of a prize panel or committee determines the result, thus signalling the inevitable subjectivity of judgement; but he then makes a point that seems closer to Middleton's heart: judges of art prizes, having been exposed to thousands of decent paintings and sculptures, can no longer 'pick out one or two that are outstanding', and so 'look around for originality, the ingredient missing from these productions' (pp. 26–7).

The analogy with the Booker Prize, if intended, misfires; but Montgomery is surely right that the effect of prize culture is to push our tastes, as consumers, more towards the unusual, the exotic, the sensational. This may not be the only reason for the gradual demise of the particular form of middlebrow provincial realism perfected by Middleton: if consumers of the serious literary novel are, largely, middlebrow denizens of the provinces, there is probably a limit to the number of times such readers wish to look into Middleton's mirror. The alternative urge in the consumer – to be enlightened through escape and entertainment – is surely another reason for the appeal of that which is 'exotic'. Yet the exotic may be found in our own time and place, and here writers like Middleton offer a corrective influence. The literary novel obliges us to recognize the cosmopolitan march of culture and society, but also to expect to see further evidence of it in the church hall, and on the village green, as provincial realism continues to evolve. We should also recognize that this is a long-term cultural shift in British society, pre-dating the post-consensus period, and the advent of literary prize culture.

3

Assimilating Multiculturalism

In the previous chapter I considered the complaint that literary prize culture, with the Booker Prize as the chief culprit, has helped fashion a form of postcolonial literature, and in a way that suggests a new cultural imperialism, dominated by commercial interests reaching out from London. The main thrust of this interpretation of postcolonial literature is that, by virtue of its distracting inauthenticity, it has had the effect of neutralizing indigenous literary expression. For commentators of this persuasion, world literature, in the manner of 'world music', has become 'an essentially false and touristic product' made for European and American markets.[1]

This debate hinges on how one understands cultural globalization. If this is viewed as something inflicted from the metropolitan centre, as the exportation of identities and interests, aestheticized for an international readership with a culturally neutral common denominator, then world literature in English, outdoing the cultural flattening of 'world music' might seem to be the literary equivalent of MTV.

Without forgetting any proper reservations about cultural globalization, however, there is an issue of necessity here that must not be overlooked: world literature is as much a response to the global moment as it is a product of it. We need also to grapple with that term 'cosmopolitanism', and learn to see it (for example) as an effect of economic migration as much as metropolitan elitism, and so a sign of new and complex global identities.

There is one British location that brings these and other related issues to a head: London's new East End. And the obvious novel to

75

consider about this location is Monica Ali's *Brick Lane* (2003), a book that has been at the centre of recent debates about ethnicity, identity and authenticity.

On publication, Ali's *Brick Lane* was condemned by some members of the Brick Lane Bengali Muslim community who found it insulting. Ian Jack had been on the panel that voted unanimously for Monica Ali to be included as one of *Granta*'s 'Best of Young British Novelists 2003', purely on the basis of the typescript for *Brick Lane*. Of the local unrest, he noted that 'for a day or two it made a story in the papers; there was a frisson of Salman Rushdie and the fatwa.' Jack speculates on two reasons why 'the Greater Sylhet Welfare and Development Council' might have objected so strongly to the novel: assuming this body to be male-dominated, he suggested that 'the novel's theme of an immigrant Muslim woman's struggle to come into her own . . . had got up their noses'. He also hints at a more local instance of ethnic conflict: since the Bangladeshis of East London 'come almost entirely from the town and district of Sylhet'; and as 'Sylhettis are seen by many other people in Bangladesh as not quite the thing'; and as neither Monica Ali nor her principal characters are from Sylhet, was there, in the anger of local Sylhettis, a complaint rooted in the issue of who is qualified to write about whom?[2]

It is Ali's marvellous comic creation, the character Chanu, who is made to voice anti-Sylhetti prejudice in the novel; and to seasoned novel readers this is patently part of Ali's characterization, a way of emphasizing Chanu's self-importance and which the reader, therefore, instinctively resists. The objections to the novel, then, raised some important questions about this supposedly 'multicultural' novel: was this a fresh instance of cultural misunderstanding, the methods of the novel writer being denounced because they were misunderstood? Or was the 'insult' really to the traditional patriarchal way of life that Ali's novel undermines, something those protesting felt inclined to fudge? And was there a self-conscious 'misunderstanding' (which had been rehearsed so thoroughly after the Rushdie affair) on the part of this community organization in pursuing its ends?

In July 2006 the media storm-in-a-teacup brewed again, this time about the filming of *Brick Lane*, when the press picked up on a fresh campaign to prevent the filming of the novel. The *Guardian* reported that 'community leaders' had 'attacked the book on its publication in 2003', finding 'a despicable insult' in the portrayal of 'Bangladeshis living in the area as backward, uneducated and unsophisticated'.[3] The campaign against the filming culminated in a protest march on a Sunday at the end of July, attended, according to one report, by 'no more than two women and 70 older men'.[4] Neither was the protest a repetition of the Bradford demonstrations at the height of the Rushdie affair: despite threats of blockades, violence and book-burning, the low-key protest featured the symbolic 'binning', rather than burning, of the novel, a considered gesture that was a far cry from the irrationality of the anti-Rushdie campaign in the late 1980s.[5]

As more than one reporter discovered, the hostility towards Ali's book and the film project was by no means uniform among the residents of Brick Lane – the protest did not represent a 'community' voice – so it is not surprising that the protestors were all but outnumbered by media. This seems to have been a self-conscious rerun of the 'racial outrage' typified by the Rushdie affair, but without the galvanizing sense of religious insult. Yet the fresh rehearsal of the racial flashpoint revealed heightened sensitivities on all sides. English PEN became involved, to protect the freedom of the writer against 'a small group of authoritarians who don't understand the nature of fiction';[6] and the film company Ruby Films, apparently on police advice, beat a retreat to the studio, thus handing a victory to the protestors. (In the press, a police spokeswoman was subsequently to deny that such advice had been given.)[7]

The sorry episode was a kind of pantomime of cultural misunderstanding, with the various players fulfilling their allotted roles. The self-appointed leader of the protest, for example, dutifully displayed ignorance of the point of novel writing (if one can trust the quotation ascribed to him): 'it's not a fiction book ... this is all lies'.[8] Yet we might wonder if there were really other motivations, apart from the convenient 'refusal' to accept fiction as fiction. The reporter for *The Hindu* found that locals were apt to repeat the allegation that 'the protest was a "publicity stunt" by a group of traders'.[9] As with the protest on the book's publication, there is the prospect that the fresh protest was mobilized by a traditional contingent in Brick Lane, chary of the theme of female emancipation in Ali's novel. That only two women attended the 'damp squib' of a protest tends to reinforce this suspicion.[10] In this interpretation of the affair, the traditionalists' repudiation of the novel as 'lies' rather than 'fiction' has more purpose: it implies a partial understanding of how novels work to promulgate ideas, and to play their part in the cultural mediation of behaviour.

The role of the media in this was also subject to scrutiny: the *Guardian* stood accused of managing 'to get up a "war of words"' between Salman Rushdie and Germaine Greer, and that certainly appeared to be so.[11] Indeed, it was Greer's *Guardian* article siding with the protestors, and Rushdie's response to it published in the same paper five days later, that really fanned the flames. Greer, accepting the protestors' point of view as representative of their community, argued that 'the community has the moral right to keep the film-makers out', since filmmakers, like novelists, usurp the reality of a community, generating (in the case of the novelist) a 'sense of invasion and betrayal'. In some respects, Greer's article appears to present this as a necessary aspect of narrative fiction, whether in film or novel: 'there is no representation without misrepresentation', she writes. Yet that 'moral right' tends to suggest, therefore, that fiction-making *per se* is a reprehensible business. What was particularly contentious, however, was Greer's placing of Monica Ali, born of an English mother and a Bangladeshi father, 'on the near side of British culture, not far from the middle':

> She writes in English and her point of view is, whether she allows herself to impersonate a village Bangladeshi woman or not, British. She has forgotten her Bengali, which she would not have done if she had wanted to remember it. When it comes to writing a novel, however, she becomes the pledge of our multi-ethnicity.[12]

However much Rushdie's response was motivated by his long-running feud with Greer (and her refusal to back him over *The Satanic Verses*), his anger about the belittling of Ali seems genuine, and gets us to the heart of the matter. There was, he argued, 'a kind of double-racism' in

Greer's portrait of Ali's ethnicity: 'to suit Greer, the British-Bangladeshi Ali is denied her heritage and belittled for her Britishness, while her British-Bangladeshi critics are denied that same Britishness, which most of them would certainly insist was theirs by right.'[13]

For me, the most interesting thing about Greer's article is the connection it makes between characters in novels and real communities: 'a character is, as it were, graven in stone', she writes; 'when you are charactered you will last for ever, or pretty nearly, but what lasts will not be you'. As a consequence, 'every individual, every community ever to be written about ... feels the same sense of invasion and betrayal.'[14] Being 'charactered' is, inevitably, a form of betrayal. It is not in the nature of fiction to portray the individuals used as inspiration in ways they would feel to be accurate or faithful. Quite so: one should not turn to *Brick Lane* for a representative portrayal of the individuals comprising the Bangladeshi community in London's East End. Yet Greer's engagement with the apparent sense of 'betrayal' seems a form of lament that the novel should fail in this regard. It certainly encouraged one correspondent to judge Ali's novel adversely, finding it 'ill informed about the culture, lives and lifestyles of the community at the centre of the work'. This correspondent regretted the furore over the film, but felt that it might at least highlight the inflated reputation of the novel, which actually relies 'almost entirely on stereotypes', and cause 'literary critics to think a little harder and become a little more informed before they make their professional judgments'.[15]

In a moment, I'll try and defend myself from this charge by delving a little deeper into the sociology of this community; but I must begin by considering, in broad terms, how this novel works. In some respects, it enacts a form of assimilation by default, summarized in the exchange between Chanu and Mrs Azad, the outspoken and domineering wife of his friend, Dr Azad:

'I'm talking about the clash between Western values and our own. I'm talking about the struggle to assimilate and the need to preserve one's identity and heritage. I'm talking about children who don't know what their identity is. I'm talking about the feelings of alienation

79

engendered by a society where racism is prevalent. I'm talking about the terrific struggle to preserve one's sanity while striving to achieve the best for one's family. I'm talking –'

'Crap! . . . Why do you make it so complicated?' said the doctor's wife. 'Assimilation this, alienation that! Let me tell you a few simple facts. Fact: we live in a Western society. Fact: our children will act more and more like Westerners. Fact: that's no bad thing.' (pp. 92–3)

Of course, assimilation is one-way traffic, whereas a vital form of multiculturalism requires something more complex and reciprocal, and Ali builds an idea of mutuality into the design of her novel by appropriating the great motor of the European novel: the love plot configured as a choice between passion and propriety. Indeed, at the heart of *Brick Lane* is a model of multiculturalism that might flow from different perceptions of love. Nazneen's emancipation is not just from the dependent role assigned to her by virtue of the arranged marriage that brings her from a village in Bangladesh to be installed in Tower Hamlets, as the bride of the pompous, excitable and ridiculous Chanu. After her passionate affair with Karim (which she decides to end), and knowing of her headstrong sister Hasina's long-term hardship in Dhaka, Nazneen rejects the fantasy of romantic love – 'we made each other up', she tells Karim (p. 380) – to embrace the bedrock of a marriage that gradually assumes a central place in her life. It is Dr Azad, reflecting tragically on his own 'love marriage', who muses on this key distinction:

> What I did not know – I was a young man – is that there are two kinds of love. The kind that starts off big and slowly wears away, that seems you can never use it up and then one day is finished. And the kind that you don't notice at first, but which adds a little bit to itself every day, like an oyster makes a pearl, grain by grain, a jewel from the sand. (p. 359)

Ali shows Nazneen and Chanu's love, nurtured by parenthood, to be of the latter kind. Notionally, she is working with an opposition between 'Western' and 'Eastern' projections of love, between romantic passion – love in 'the English style' as Nazneen's friend Razia has it (p. 358) – and the dutiful love that is expected in an arranged marriage. Yet, over this apparent opposition, Ali overlays a staple moral theme of the English novel: the choice between the grand passion and the sensible romantic alliance, and here the East–West opposition breaks down. This is important, because the novel is then not simply allowing Nazneen to choose the traditional way, having been exposed to the Western alternative (though that is part of the point); it is also demonstrating that, over the question of romantic love, there is no cultural divide. We are presented with a love plot predicated on the East–West cultural clash, and resolved paradoxically so that the emancipated principal chooses the notional path of oppression, which is thereby demythologized in this case. Yet we are also invited to see how this maps onto a longstanding tradition of social mores in the English novel, where the sensible alliance is invariably promoted over the path of reckless desire. This is the genuine multicultural gesture in this fine and moving novel, an incremental contribution to the evolution of the cultural form.

Ali, it should be acknowledged, cheerfully uses *types* to advance a positive political message of integration, and this further fuels the charge that the characters in the novel are unrepresentative. How can this charge be answered? This first point to reiterate is that this is often the case in novels that engage our interest. It is also worth observing, however, that the complaint is really nonsensical, taken to its logical conclusion, since it requires of the novelist the kind of sociological knowledge and range that is not his or her business. This is another of those extraordinary expectations that actually reveal the high esteem in which the novel is held, since it is looked to to produce an extensive mode of representation that is inevitably beyond its reach. Such criticisms tacitly acknowledge the power and scope of the novelistic imagination, while highlighting for us its necessary limitations.

In the case of *Brick Lane*, there are some notable comic creations (rather than 'stereotypes'): the sinister Mrs Islam, for instance, the hypochondriac matriarch who is revealed as a usurer, and who is faced down by Nazneen in a memorable scene, where Nazneen insists that Mrs Islam, if she wants another payment on the 'loan' secured by Nazneen's husband, must swear on a copy of the Qur'an that she has not been charging interest (p. 371). (She cannot do so, of course.) Best of all is Chanu, Nazneen's husband, who begins as a self-congratulating but deluded failure, to become a loving, but broken man. Ultimately, he is the novel's most sympathetic character – a Pooter who develops self-knowledge – and a very remarkable invention.

The question of representation, and the selectivity that necessarily informs the conception of a single novel, evidently becomes more contentious in the depiction of marginalized ethnic groups, putting a special constraint on the writer who chooses to represent such groups. To assess how far this is a legitimate concern in reading *Brick Lane*, it will be helpful to have points of comparison, beyond the realm of fiction. Useful, here, is the treatment offered by another 'outsider', Tarquin Hall, whose *Salaam Brick Lane: A Year in the New East End* (2005) makes for an intriguing companion piece, and which reads like an autobiographical novel.[16] Returning to London with no money, after ten years abroad working as a freelance journalist, Hall finds himself renting a dilapidated attic flat in Brick Lane, a far cry from the leafy suburb of Barnes, where he had grown up. His experiences in the new East End define him as an outsider, both to the multi-ethnic community of Brick Lane and to the white East Enders. Indeed, the greatest hostility comes from this quarter, notably when a friend takes Hall to a local pie and mash shop, the better 'to soak up some good old Cockney atmosphere'. However, the pair of them are subjected to the taunts of the other customers, who associate them with the various economic threats to their existence, and who speak loudly about 'toffee-nosed yuppies moving in' (p. 48).

Hall strikes up closer links with the multi-ethnic community: he is befriended by his Sylheti landlord, Mr Ali, and establishes friendships with asylum seekers from Afghanistan and Kosovo, and with an elderly Jewish neighbour. However, his most interesting acquaintance, from the point of view of understanding multiculturalism, is Aktar, a West Bengali intellectual, who is making a study of the East End's Bangladeshi population. He enlists Hall's help when he wishes to turn his attention to the 'indigenous white population', and this episode becomes the focus of the book's treatment of multiculturalism.

Aktar's attitudes are important in this connection. Having been drawn to England as a young man in the 1960s, 'in awe of British literature and academia', he is shocked by modern-day London, which he finds permeated by American culture. In his view, 'Western liberalism encourages a great many activities and attitudes which, from an anthropological perspective, may be termed primitive' (p. 155).

With some difficulty, Hall arranges a series of interviews within the 'indigenous white population', but, to Aktar's growing dismay, the interviewees all turn out to have hybrid ethnic backgrounds. In the first household they visit, the wife claims to be 'one quarta gypsy' on her father's side, and to have Irish ancestry on her mother's side (p. 225). The story is repeated in the five other households they visit, where ancestors are unearthed from Malta, Sicily, Scotland, Wales, the Caribbean, and other regions of England. Aktar feels his study will be compromised if he cannot find people who are 'one hundred per cent English' (p. 225); and, seeking to placate him, Hall comes up with the idea of visiting the Harvest Festival to be held by 'the last of the real Cockneys, the Pearly Kings and Queens' (p. 227). Of course, the pursuit of racial purity is thwarted here, too, in the person of a Pearly Princess with a West Indian father (p. 230). Aktar, however, has already learned the lesson, having discovered the fluid etymology and generalized meaning of the term 'Cockney': 'who is to say what a Cockney might be in the future? Perhaps even the descendants of the Bangladeshi community will one day be considered true Londoners. It seems that here in London anything is possible' (p. 229).

Aktar's conclusions about the Bangladeshi community seem sound enough: he feels 'the younger generation were fast shedding the values and interests of their grandparents and parents and adopting a "hybrid identity."' He perceives a pattern to be repeating itself, where economic forces draw an immigrant group into British culture: 'Throughout the East End's history, every immigrant group that has settled has been seized by this entrepreneurial spirit: from the Huguenots to the Jews and so on' (p. 219). This is really the heart of Hall's presentation about multiculturalism in the East

End; it has provided a foothold for successive waves of immigrants, starting at the bottom of society in economic terms, who have worked to escape to more salubrious environs. Hall's year in the East End replicates the experience in miniature: returning to London as an impoverished 'outsider'. With his Indian-American fiancée, he endures the hardships of Brick Lane until financial circumstances enable them to escape to Dalston, 'traditionally a step up for Cockneys escaping the East End proper' (p. 251), but with designs on Stoke Newington (p. 264).

This emphasis on Brick Lane as a transitional space for the migrant settler inspires Jeremy Gavron's *An Acre of Barren Ground* (2005), a fictionalized 'archaeology' of Brick Lane, written as a series of vignettes across history, in the manner of Adam Thorpe's *Ulverton*, so that some of the episodes are cross-referenced with each other. The history of different immigrant East End communities – Jews, Huguenots, Bangladeshis – is conveyed effectively by this method, which is extended to the treatment of well-known historical figures (such as Boswell and Jack the Ripper), and even to animals, including a tormented performing bear.

A contemporary focus is supplied by the reference to 9/11 in the story of Willy Wilson, who is presented as an acquaintance of the author. Wilson, 'the canary trainer', is a loner of a fragile mental state, whose character is defined for us by a formative episode in the 1960s when he fell in with some racist thugs. Taunted by them, he attacks a man of Pakistani origin, apparently to repudiate the suggestion of his similarity to his victim. Gavron, announced as the narrator of this section, remarks: 'that was the moment, in my mind, that the young Willy of my imagination turned into the old Willy I used to see in the market. Shrunk in size, and shrunk into himself' (p. 318). Wilson's decline is then figured as a culmination of all the horrors of the modern age: the decimated East End of his wartime childhood, the atomic bomb, 'asteroids, plague, this global warming, and most recently, this terrorism'. The images of the planes flying into the World Trade Centre 'excited him in a way nothing had done for years', somehow persuading him to let his birds go, shortly before his own death (p. 319).

This episode, placed near the end of the novel, implies something apocalyptic about 'this terrorism'; but also a culmination of human cruelty in which Willy has participated, through his brief (and presumably shaming) flirtation with racism. This is not a book that celebrates the diversity of human flourishing as a conscious fact of the life lived. Rather, diversity emerges as a fact of historical accident and circumstance, through successive waves of ethnic change. Within this diversity, cruelty, suffering and poverty are presented as the normal conditions of existence.

Gavron's novel moves in the opposite direction to most contemporary accounts of multiculturalism, which are usually haunted by the problem of integration. Tarquin Hall offers his own thoughts on this, apropos of an encounter with his fiancée's 'auntie', Mrs Suri, who is seeking to break up their relationship by arranging an alternative husband. He considers her hostility to British culture to be hypocritical, a way of denying 'the individualism that had allowed her to prosper in the UK in the first place'. He goes on:

> As much as I was for immigrants settling in the UK, I saw integration as imperative. After all, if I raised my own children in India as staunch Brits, eating fish and chips, saluting the Queen and warning them not to become too Indian, I would rightly be ostracized. (p. 118)

The trajectory of Hall's narrative serves to soften and to complicate this position; but the thought – raised in anger at this point – raises key questions about integration that are worth considering. Of course, were Hall to raise a family in India, the situation would not be directly equivalent to that of an Indian family settling in Britain. The legacy of imperialism would certainly establish very different contexts, even if there were no economic differences of circumstance. Yet this simplified 'when in Rome' version of integration has the air of an impregnable 'common sense' that is sometimes insensitive to context.

It is also insensitive to the dynamics of biological and cultural hybridity that the book shows to be inevitable on the basis of its snapshot of East End demographics. That 'insensitivity', however, is established as something more troubling, since, in its 'flipside', it becomes a form of cultural appropriation, a trait of national identity with its roots in imperialism: Aktar remarks to Hall:

> you English . . . are unique in that you loot elements of other cultures and then you make them your own. For want of a better word, you 'English' them. And in so doing, you somehow convince yourselves that whatever it is that you have absorbed was English in the first place. Then you go one step further and present it to the world as such. (p. 246)

These concerns about cultural appropriation seem inconsequential, however, in the face of those forces implacably opposed to any form of integration. Perhaps the most troubling aspect of Hall's book is the hostility of the section of the community designated as white British, and which sees itself as such despite its evident hybridization. The hostility extends to both monied interlopers and to immigrants, and in both cases the source of the perceived grievance is economic. This analysis is confirmed in an important sociological study by Geoff Dench, Kate Gavron and Michael Young, *The New East End: Kinship, Race and Conflict* (2006).[17] The survey is based on interviews conducted in the 1990s, from 1992 onwards; but it has a currency, and chimes with Tarquin Hall's findings. Indeed, Dench, Gavron and Young find the conversations reported in Hall's narrative to be 'reminiscent of our interviews of between five and ten years earlier, with a few exceptions', the chief one being that the sociologists' interviewees had made little mention of the drug problem that Hall found to be rife.

Their conclusions tally with the impetus of Hall's views about economics, and the East End being a focus of entrepreneurial effort. Indeed, with perceived white grievances in mind, they make a plea against an interventionist approach to the problem of conflict. In a laudable attempt to understand what fuels racism (rather than simply denouncing it out of hand), Dench, Gavron and Young point out that their 'white informants have a perception that nothing is being done for them and plenty – too much, even – is being done for

86

others'. However muddled they may be, such grievances quite properly inform the study's conclusion. Here the authors argue that 'informal moral economies' give people 'some stake in the system', and that 'over-centralization of welfare in the name of strict equality is stifling this'. This argument for community based moral responsibility has a particular importance for new immigrants: 'if you take away the need to make an effort, and integrate many newcomers straight into a state-dependent underclass, then nobody wins.'

There is, however, an implicit plea for some form of steady change – an incremental form of integration – in this conclusion. During their fieldwork, the authors observed that 'the last Jewish shops and organizations in the area' were closing down, having sustained the Jewish descendants of nineteenth-century immigrants until the end of the twentieth century. This observation about how long it has taken, historically, for a community 'to leave its base in the East End' is used to reflect on the Bangladeshi community, and how state intervention may be helping Bangladeshis to settle and, in some cases, 'to move on quickly', thus eroding the community base they need. This may be one reason, they speculate, in a dark allusion to the London bombings of 7 July 2005, why government policy colludes with the most serious problem of non-integration today: 'already by the middle of 2005 it was becoming obvious how potentially dangerous even a small number of young men could be who feel alienated from and antagonistic to the rest of the country. Too-speedy dissolution of the ethnic community could multiply these risks.'[18]

From a political point of view, the notion of a stabilized community would seem to be efficacious only if it is also a point of cultural and ethnic intersection. The novel can deliver snapshots of such points of intersection; and this suggests an important social function for works sometimes dismissed as idealistic or unrepresentative. Here the novel reveals its potential to play a constructive role, a role that is now much diminished. In a lucid essay on 'new ethnicities', James Proctor, following Stuart Hall, pinpoints the moment in the late 1980s when ethnic difference begins to be promoted by black artists, 'as "black" ceased to operate as a unifying collective category';

embodied in this moment is the 'recognition that representation plays a formative, constitutive role', beyond its simply mimetic function.[19]

By the time Ali's *Brick Lane* was published in 2003, however, and especially after the enthusiastic reception of Zadie Smith's *White Teeth* in 2000, literary critics were beginning to wonder whether or not the commodification of multicultural London was becoming politically regressive. The rationality of this seems to me to be questionable. If those writers once deemed to be of 'ethnic minority' status no longer felt obliged to promote 'black' interests in an oppositional manner, their art, empowered to pursue an exploratory and formative celebration of difference, was freed from being a form of anti-racist propaganda. As the trend developed, such writers inevitably became mainstream, and this is surely a very important development in contemporary British culture.

The question that has been raised, however, is whether or not there is a degree of complicity between postcolonial literatures, and, in Graham Huggan's words, 'the global late-capitalist system in which these discourses circulate and are contained'. Huggan is especially interested in the complex 'relations between contemporary postcolonial studies and the booming "alterity industry" that it at once serves and resists'. The central charge that Huggan considers is this: 'postcolonial studies, it could be argued, has capitalized on its perceived marginality while helping turn marginality itself into a valuable intellectual commodity.'[20] Proctor wonders if this might also be true of 'books like *Brick Lane* and *White Teeth*', in an implication that the celebration of difference in British culture might have tipped over into a cynical *marketing* of it.

In his account of *Brick Lane*, Proctor acknowledges the way in which Ali 'refuses to present characters as mouthpieces for a political vision', and the implications this refusal has for our reception of the novel. He also focuses on the degree to which 'Nazneen has acquired an empowering degree of agency' by the conclusion; but he finds something troubling in the entrepreneurship that establishes her independence, 'working in partnership with Fusion Fashions, a trendy white-run clothes store that plies the kind of fashionable ethnic chic the novel elsewhere appears to deprecate.' Proctor considers this to be 'an odd kind of emancipatory ending' because 'it has little to offer in the way of political alternatives'; yet he acknowledges that the novel 'clearly disrupts certain conventional ways of representing race, racism, and identity in productive ways'.[21] This last is well said, and identifies the very considerable achievement of Ali's novel.

It is worth noting that the 'fashionable ethnic chic' that Nazneen works to promote seems to be a deliberate parallel of the cultural globalization to which *Brick Lane* contributes: Ali, in inviting the parallel, is pre-empting her critics and acknowledging the inevitability of the commercial parameters within which her work will have to function.

We should also consider, however, the expectation of a 'political alternative', which may be beyond the scope of most novels. Entrepreneurship, in the guise of local business enterprise, has historically been the means of self-assertion for East End immigrants, and also the means through which they have generated the requisite capital to move away, so there is a basis in verisimilitude for Ali in her presentation of a new ethnic rag trade. As we have seen, the sociologists Dench, Gavron and Young consider the emphasis on financial self-help also to be the best means of establishing the moral economy necessary for interim community stability in the East End (against the policies of a modernizing and centralizing government), so Ali's ending is in tune, at least, with this 'political alternative'.

When one considers *Brick Lane* as a post-9/11 novel, there is a very clear political dimension to Nazneen's emancipation, which is both private and public. An impressive aspect of *Brick Lane*, in fact, is the manner in which the events of 9/11 are related to the lives of the characters, and the direction of Ali's plot. Nazneen's horror at the spectacle of someone trapped and jumping from one of the Twin Towers (p. 305) recalls her earlier fascination, when she is new to England, with the story of the apparent suicide of a woman, jumping from her flat, sixteen floors up. The rumour mongers had reflected on the hapless woman's childless marriage – 'the worst thing for any woman' – hinting that the husband may have had a hand in the 'accident' (p. 20). This figure of cultural alienation and imprisonment, as a shadow of possibility for Nazneen, is already dispelled by 2001, but is definitively recast by the terrorist suicides of 9/11. Suicide looms large in her mind after 9/11, and, despite Karim's talk of martyrs, she feels the dictum that 'a Muslim cannot commit suicide' to be incontrovertible (p. 318). Hasina's letter of October 2001 confirms that their oppressed mother's fatal accident had actually been suicide (p. 364), and this revelation is tied in to Nazneen's gathering forcefulness and determination to make the most of her life: in one sense, the spirit of her emancipation stands in opposition to the death-wish, and this clearly has a pointed significance when lauded as the resolve of a Muslim woman in Britain, 2001.

The novel's plot turns on the events of 9/11, as the two camps of the radical Muslim organization – one wishing to concentrate on opposing racism locally, the other wishing to mobilize for jihad abroad – are thrown into violent conflict, which turns out to be cathartic, since the tardy local authorities are shocked into a community-building brief. Chanu determines, finally, to go back to Bangladesh; and Nazneen is galvanized with a new mood of self-assertion, breaking things off with Karim, standing up to Mrs Islam, and determining to defy Chanu and stay with her daughters in England. It also seems to be the immediate 9/11 context that prompts Hasina to write to Nazneen, revealing the truth about their mother's death. The projection of two global tribes is also defied by Nazneen: in latching on to the outlawing of suicide in Islam, she makes her own 'pro-life' gesture, a personal act of self-determination that exorcises her mother's ghost. At the same time, she rejects the terrorists' two-tribes mentality.

Nazneen's resistance of the new post-9/11 tribalism, which also asserts her distance from her mother's suffering, is the source of her hard-won independence. Rather than an instance of cultural assimilation, we can read this as a more benign form of integration, in which the abiding independent spirit of East End immigration supplies the bedrock for a newly politicized Muslim identity.

The instant-celebrity status of Monica Ali, however, like that of Zadie Smith, is now often seen as a symptom of what Mark Stein calls 'containment': 'by concentrating disproportionately on a small number of recognizable voices, post-colonial polyphony is in danger of being muffled'. It is 'the media, the book trade' that Stein castigates to explain how 'the breadth and heterogeneity of black British cultural production' is overlooked; but he is also concerned with a form of institutionalized delusion in this regard:

> In celebrating black and Asian writers, Britain also celebrates its own 'official' multiculturalism and in this way affiliates itself with diversity. With the British Council, for example, supporting a range of British writers from ethnic minorities, alongside writers from the Commonwealth, the image of an open, tolerant, and quintessentially mixed society is exported.[22]

The objection raises the spectre of an unattainable purity, impervious to the selectivity necessary in any cultural practice. Of greater concern is the effect of such ideas when they gain currency, and produce distorting impressions. For example, academic critics may have become accustomed to the idea that the celebrity status of writers like Monica Ali and Zadie Smith is conferred upon them by virtue of how their version of multicultural London appeals to (and is somehow exotic for) a white middlebrow readership. To the extent that this is true, I see no particular reason to condemn the encounter between such a readership and an idealized representation of multicultural life. This is, surely, an advance on the invisibility of multiculturalism in the mainstream serious novel until very recently. And while it is certainly true that only a tiny percentage of 'multicultural' writers are widely read, this is true of all novelists and all genres, and need not be taken as a form of implicit racism: the 'stifling' of the true range of the multicultural novel is also true, surely, of the regional novel, the campus novel, the sink estate novel. It is, I suspect, as much a mark of blind competition, as it is an indication of engineering or design.

The ethnic diversity reflected in the work of the British Council – a form of artificiality that may be discernible in any university reading list of postcolonial writing as well – may also be more benign than we might fear. Such activities may not actually build a false image of an open, tolerant and mixed society. Rather, the self-conscious promotion of multicultural writing is surely an instance of a kind of hopeful defensiveness: we may have racism, intolerance, tribalism and the violence they spawn; but we do, at least, have a handful of novels celebrating an alternative multicultural experience, written by novelists whose prominence attests to a cultural advance. The perceived problem may be manufactured by the expectation that the novel should have delivered more than this.

Like Proctor, Stein is influenced in his deliberations by Graham Huggan, whose sophisticated argument is rooted in the idea that complicity is unavoidable, for both the postcolonial writer and critic, and that a form of 'strategic exoticism' has emerged as a consequence. In this account, postcolonial writers (and thinkers), having to work 'within exoticist codes of representation', find ways of subverting these codes, or succeed in redeploying them for the purposes of uncovering differential relations of power. Agency is severely restricted, however, because 'the self-conscious use of exoticist techniques' can be understood as a further symptom of 'the postcolonial exotic' rather than a response to it.[23]

Once again, the debate turns on how the question of cosmopolitanism is understood. Writers who are taken to be representative of ethnic minority cultures are invariably seen to be not 'of' those cultures, but, rather, part of a new cultural elite. Yet this has not diminished their role in mainstream debates about national identity. Several critics have noted that, in the words of Tobias Wachinger, 'writers like Hanif Kureishi, David Dabydeen and, most recently, Zadie Smith are at the forefront, rather than the periphery, of contemporary debates about Britishness'.

Yet Wachinger's main concern is the 'cultural politics' that 'steers the negotiation between "in-between" writer and dominantly metropolitan readership'.[24] Pertinent here is Timothy Brennan's definition of a new cosmopolitanism in the era of globalization, because it articulates a cultural trend that is seen to be complicitous with the expanding world model of capitalist democracy. Yet this cosmopolitanism is richly ambivalent, even while being somehow imprisoning, embracing 'celebratory claims and despairing recognitions', and involving questions of national identity, transculturation and consumerism.

For Brennan, there is a troubling relationship between globalization and the cultural understanding of cosmopolitanism because 'the contemporary discourse of globalism entails the theorization of a subject – a social type – to give it scope'.[25] America is Brennan's chief concern, yet the implications of this account of cosmopolitanism must reach beyond the US, since it identifies a global type, appropriated in the interests of capital. For Wachinger, for example, Brennan's concern that terms like 'cosmopolitanism' and 'hybridity' are emptied of their significance informs his account of the problematic 'in-between' migrant writer, 'a privileged figure', who 'can rely on a ready availability of identity positions'. The impetus of Wachinger's work, indeed, is to anatomize the identity of the migrant writer 'writing from a "space-in-between"' in such a way that 'both Englishness and Otherness are reinforced, rather than destabilized'. Rather than the route to genuine hybridity, or a vital form of multiculturalism, therefore, 'the insider/outsider position proves not much more than a self-ingratiating cosmopolitan fantasy which has to be understood in relation to the ideological and institutional structures in which it is housed'. A question to consider is, if this is sometimes true of the migrant writer's identity – and it is the identity projected by publishers' marketing machinery that usually exercises critics – does it *determine* how we interpret the novels of these writers?

Turning his attention to Zadie Smith, Wachinger finds it 'disturbing' that *White Teeth* 'advertises its own status as product of the "space-in-between"': moreover, the sterility of the marketing context infects the writer's self-consciousness, in his reading: 'Smith seems to know all too well that the "in-between" position is likely to prove a condition of (comic) entrapment and (self-parodic) repetition.'[26]

I think we have to accept that, for most readers, there is some element of elision between the writer's public persona and the appeal of his or her work, though the degree to which that elision influences how readers interpret novels may not be particularly significant. The charge here, however, is that the ideological imprisonment that goes with being the latest multicultural sensation reduces the writing to a kind of pantomime of identity, a far cry from the exploratory performance that might contribute to the forging of new identities.

Elsewhere I have suggested precisely the contrary view, that Smith's novel can be read as an instance of the reforging of nationhood in Homi Bhabha's terms, where an authoritative 'pedagogic' tendency in perceptions of national identity comes into productive tension with a 'performative' process of reconstruction.[27]

Is this judgement in need of revision in the post-9/11 context? Certainly, *White Teeth* has an innocence that is inconceivable now, though the novel is very clear in its treatment of Islamic extremism, and the appeal of extremism to some young British Asians: the motives of the character Millat, participating in the Bradford book-burning at the height of the Rushdie Affair, are shown to be contradictory and irrational, yet explicable in the face of the racist interpellation and ethnic suppression suffered by people like him (p. 202). The naivety of the novel, if such it is, has not to do with its misunderstanding of racial tension, however, but with its celebration of transcultural hybridity. Yet this is a form of willed and self-conscious celebration, caught up in the spirit of a positive end-of-millennium moment. Cultural hybridity, within given social and economic limits, is shown to be a contradictory, haphazard, and yet inevitable phenomenon; and if this seems facile in summary, it is an idea that produces an extravagant comic novel, with an array of characters who occasionally get a little too close to caricature – but that is a familiar danger, and a venial sin in the comic novelist.

In one of the more didactic moments in *White Teeth*, Smith celebrates rootlessness, a celebration of postcolonial migration that has inevitably drawn comparisons with Rushdie, the figurehead of a new postcolonial cosmopolitanism. Indeed, Rushdie's career supplies a way of focusing migration and cosmopolitanism, and the problem of articulating its significance. There is now something approaching a consensus that his two best books are *Midnight's Children* (1981) and *Shame* (1983), both highly political novels – the former an allegory about India, the latter a satire about Pakistan – in which the narrative engagement with character was not supplanted by the political message, nor by the writer's self-consciousness. Rushdie, on the basis of these works, was installed as the key exponent of a global form of migrant writing, a position (and a condition) that was highly unstable.

Since then, Rushdie has frequently been criticized for his over-ambitiousness, and his tendency to hyperbole, attributes that are both evident in his recent *Shalimar the Clown* (2005), a post-9/11 novel that tries to engage with the mind-set of a terrorist, and with the problem of Kashmir, in a manner that some reviewers felt to be another instance of the later Rushdie's failing: his tendency to allow the political to supplant the personal.[28]

Although the reassessment of Rushdie is partly justified, there is also something contradictory within it. After all, we should expect his writing to change in response to new circumstances, and to explain the change we may need to resist the temptation to suggest that he now relies on the recycling of old tricks that become too prominent.[29] Indeed, the change that has assailed Rushdie is a shifting perception of globalization, a topic that he engages explicitly in *Shalimar the Clown*: 'Everywhere was now a part of everywhere else. Russia, America, London, Kashmir. Our lives, our stories, flowed into one another's, were no longer our own, individual, discrete. This unsettled people. There were collisions and explosions. The world was no longer calm' (p. 37).

Does this element of self-consciousness diminish the work? For the *TLS* reviewer, it signals a fundamental flaw, since the acceptance of a global readership results in a pandering to a low artistic common denominator: 'the global novel must appeal to the greatest number', and so must supply 'spectacle' in 'homage' to film, 'the new master art form'. For that reviewer, Rushdie makes a disastrous choice in doing so: 'rather than explore the crossing points between Western civilization which aestheticizes violence and Islamic civilizations which sanctify it, Rushdie writes himself in on the side of the aestheticizers.'[30]

Of course, to register global tendencies in a novel may be to ironize rather than to ape them; and we may also wonder if a certain degree of aestheticization is inevitable in the novelistic treatment of violence. There was at least one British reviewer prepared to see in the novel an imaginative engagement 'with the shock of 11 September 2001 and the wars that have followed'.[31] The example of *Shalimar the Clown* reveals the vulnerability of the writer who is expected to engage with global multicultural questions, and the concomitant feeling that there is no particular *community* to be served by such a writer, other than the elite 'community' of migrant writers. Yet the role of such a writer may be to shake up our notions of community in the first place.

Literary critics are often disappointed by the failure of novelists to portray community convincingly. A question to ponder, however, is whether or not a novel can realize a satisfying or complete vision of community. Would such a work be readable as a novel? Again, our critical habits, which lead us to expect remarkable things, can also lead us to fault novelists for failing to realize the impossible. Can we expect our novelists to produce the concrete vision of *purposive* globalization that has eluded all other forms of discourse and human endeavour? To me, the transitional work commonly associated with Rushdie and other postcolonial writers is more than enough to expect of the novel, and more than enough to discuss in novel criticism.

For the literary critic, it is a shock to turn from postcolonial literary theory, where the idea of cosmopolitanism is usually rejected as a malign effect of late capitalism, to the growing body of work on cosmopolitanism written by political scientists and moral philosophers. In these fields, the cosmopolitan identity often emerges as our single main resource of hope in combating the worst effects of globalization; and the novel is sometimes deemed to be a useful instrument in that endeavour. Is it possible that the austere and exacting political expectations of postcolonial literary theorists serve, at times, to disregard the possibilities that reside in the literary response?

Kwame Anthony Appiah's projection of cosmopolitan values, as an ethical imperative, is rooted in the cultivation of 'a form of universalism that is sensitive to the ways in which historical context may shape the significance of a practice'. With regard to the novel, it is 'an invitation to respond in imagination to narratively constructed situations' that is crucial. The novel demonstrates that 'what makes the cosmopolitan experience possible for us, whether as readers or as travellers', is the 'narrative logic that allows us to construct the world to which our imaginations respond.' For Appiah, 'this is the moral epistemology that makes cosmopolitanism possible.'[32] As the next chapter demonstrates, this imaginative capacity is now under particular pressure.

It seems indisputable that the novel, with its central reliance on empathy with individual identity, and the reader's faith in the idea of selfhood, partakes of the 'liberalism' Appiah defines, where 'identity is at the heart of human life'. Yet this is more than a valueless capacity. Where the 'cosmopolitan impulse' is appended to this liberalism, 'cultural and social variety' become the 'precondition for the self-creation that is at the heart of a meaningful human life.' This reveals an important pragmatism, since this concept of cosmopolitanism links human variety directly with human agency.[33]

To unleash the potential of the novel in Britain, however, adherents to such a theory of cosmopolitanism will need to be more sanguine about the role of publishing conglomerates, and the processes of cultural globalization, than postcolonial critics have tended to be, hitherto. Such critics will inevitably need to attend to that 'new form of cosmopolitanism' observed by Bruce King, that emerged in the 1990s, and which saw writers from other countries increasingly inclined to use England as a base, with the ease of international travel, and the attraction of the 'publishing and literary worlds' focused on London. The resulting 'large community of resident writers from elsewhere' comprised a new type, 'neither immigrants nor birds of passage', but 'resident migrants'. The challenge is to see how this narrower form of literary cosmopolitanism feeds in to Appiah's conception of agency.

In King's account of how 'the globalization of the world's economy' extends and supersedes decolonization, 'the internationalization of English literature' – with English becoming the world's predominant language in the period that 'an American ideology of free trade' rises to pre-eminence – is, inevitably, part of a new world liberalism. King's stress on entrepreneurship in publishing links the work of the writer to other kinds of work in 'a globalized economy' with a discernible 'internationalization of the marketplace'.[34]

The confluence of these economic and political forces explains why postcolonial critics have been so sceptical about the construction of the multicultural writer in Britain. Yet we can also rely, perhaps, on a staple feature of literary theory to circumvent the idea of an imprisoning context: the idea of relative autonomy. The autonomy of the literary response puts in perspective the idea that the marketing hype that launches a Zadie Smith or a Monica Ali carves out an exotic niche, artificially inscribed. And the question of audience is important here, too. Novel readers at the beginning of the twenty-first century do not comprise a homogeneous group for whom such a notion of ethnic difference could have an exotic appeal; which suggests that the success of the hype has surely more to do with the perceived importance of multiculturalism as a topic, for both publishers and readers. There are sound reasons for celebrating this success.

4

Terrorism in Transatlantic
Perspective

In the previous chapter my discussion of postcolonial and multicultural issues intersected, inevitably, with the attack on America in September 2001. That event and its aftermath is the central focus of this chapter, which seeks to investigate whether or not 9/11 really does mark out a moment of cultural change, and a new era of literary history.

In a provocative article about the future of the novel, published in the wake of 9/11, James Wood sounded the death-knell of the social novel in its current conception: the idea 'that the novelist's task is to go on to the street and figure out social reality', he suggested, 'may well have been altered by the events of September 11, merely through the reminder that whatever the novel gets up to, the "culture" can always get up to something bigger.' Ostensibly, Wood was attacking 'the dream of the Great American Social Novel', the tradition of John Dos Passos and Sinclair Lewis, 'revivified by Don DeLillo's *Underworld*'. It is an approach that demands a wealth of social knowledge in the novelist trying 'to pin down an entire writhing culture'.[1]

Wood was also responding to New York novelist Jay McInerney's account of 9/11, and his remark to Bret Easton Ellis about the difficulty he will have in returning to work on his novel-in-progress, set in 'the very New York that has just been altered for ever'.[2] Wood's spleen is partly directed against the trivial 'New York novel' he feels to be epitomized by McInerney. Yet the net he casts draws in other kinds of novels and novelists – including the exuberant multiculturalism of

99

Zadie Smith, who had published *White Teeth* in 2000. The 'Social Novel' he constructs is a broad target, with a transatlantic resonance. The various tendencies it identifies stand in opposition to the trend he would like to see more of, involving 'novels that tell us not "how the world works" but "how somebody felt about something"'.[3]

There is a sense in which novelists, post-9/11, have moved in the direction Wood identified as desirable, and this greater emphasis on personal feeling has involved a discernible shift towards the domestic sphere. Yet one of the ideas this chapter seeks to test or qualify is that 9/11 marks a watershed in literary history, or at least the end of a particularly confident phase, legitimately characterized as the internationalization of the novel in English. That turn to domestic topics in the work of prominent novelists in Britain and the US – even in books about 9/11 – seems to confirm the impression of a turning away from the full political implications of global terrorism. That may also signal a halt to the confident march towards internationalism or cosmopolitanism. It is worth bearing in mind, however, that earlier novelistic treatments of terrorism have consistently struggled with the mind-set of the terrorist, finding the limits of the discourse of the novel to be revealed by the encounter. Even so, the sense of writers having been noticeably silenced by 9/11 chimes with a global sense of taking stock – for academics too – so the event uncovers some important intellectual common ground in the broader literary culture. It also invites a comparison between fiction in Britain and the US, and such a comparison underpins the readings in this chapter.

A British novelist who had a novel in progress at the time of 9/11, and who is noted for writing on the kind of large canvas disparaged by Wood, is Martin Amis. *Yellow Dog* (2003) was some years in the making: indeed, Amis began work on it five years before publication, but 'laid it aside to absorb the death of his father and write his own memoirs'. He reports coming back to it, refreshed, on 10 September 2001, 'then the event happened and, like every other writer on earth, the next day I was considering a change in occupation'.[4] Why was it that so many novelists printed their immediate responses to 9/11? A rose-tinted view might incline us to imagine that newspaper editors consciously solicited the views of those professionally attuned to reflection on human dilemmas, hoping for copy with fresh insight. Amis's explanation is more mundane, and brings us back to the sense of impasse felt generally by novelists, and to Wood's opposing trends: 'I can tell you what those novelists were doing: they were playing for time. The so-called work in progress had been reduced, overnight, to a blue streak of pitiable babble.'

Amis's explanation for the writer feeling 'stalled' also contrasts with Wood's, however. Working through the familiar cabbalistic view (amongst novelists) that 'imaginative writing' is 'very mysterious', since 'a great deal of the work gets done beneath the threshold of consciousness, without the intercession of reason', Amis argues for the rationality that underpins the creativity:

> When the novelists went into newsprint about September 11, there was a murmur to the effect that they were now being obliged to snap out of their solipsistic daydreams: to attend, as best they could, to the facts of life. For politics – once defined as 'what's going on' – suddenly filled the sky. True, novelists don't normally write about what's going on; they write about what's not going on. Yet the worlds so created aspire to pattern and shape and moral point. A novel is a rational undertaking; it is reason at play, perhaps, but it is still reason.[5]

Like Wood, Amis recognizes the rude intrusion of politics into the world of the novel; but unlike Wood, this is not, for Amis, a question of reality exposing the hubris of the social novel. In highlighting the distinctive 'pattern and shape and moral point' – or, the 'rational undertaking' of the novel – he is articulating a purpose for it that might prioritize the 'how somebody felt about something' even against the backdrop of 'how the world works'.

Finally, this is the balance achieved in *Yellow Dog*. Amis's account of overcoming the 9/11 impasse, however, suggests he was driven by the public agenda, and an emerging bipolar view of the world:

> The fighting spirit said let's go back to the novel but also let's resolve that it is going to be a comic novel. The values that were attacked on the day were very much values such as reason and civilization. There was also the possibility of humour after an enormous blow like that. Reason and humour are indivisible.[6]

It is the broader canvas that also seems to be clearly privileged in any adequate summary of *Yellow Dog*. Neither is this surprising given the trajectory of Amis's career. Since his collection of stories *Einstein's Monsters* (1987), on the subject of nuclear proliferation and the threat of human extinction, his fiction has been dominated by apocalyptic themes. One could go back further, and argue that since *Money* (1984), with its angry and urgent treatment of greed and global capitalism in the Reagan–Thatcher era, Amis's imagination has been dominated by forms of catastrophe on a grand scale.

Yellow Dog (2003) puts typical 'Amisian' concerns – broadly concerning the larger consequences of masculine violence – self-consciously into the post-9/11 context. Three plot strands are interwoven. First, there is the story of Xan Meo, a writer and entertainer, whose personality is changed after a blow to the head by criminal henchmen. Then there is the comic story of the Royal Family, in an alternative line of descent, with Henry IX on the throne, wrestling with a blackmailer who has a compromising film of his pubescent daughter. Finally, there is the story of Clint Smoker, the epitome of the 'yellow' journalist, employed to write misogynistic bile for a pornographic daily, *The Morning Lark*. All three strands are brought together through the person of Joseph Andrews, a former East End villain, but now a pornographer living in California: he is behind the beating of Xan (who turns out to be his son); he is the Royal blackmailer (but also a sentimental Royalist, true to stereotype, as a tough East Ender); and he is killed by Clint Smoker in a finale of gruesome violence.[7]

The particular context, however, is signalled by a fourth strand concerning a comet, and a stricken airliner, which is eventually brought down by the corpse of a cuckolded husband (Royce Traynor), loose in the hold, apparently seeking vengeance on his wife and her lover (the plane's captain), who are both on board. For some readers, this fourth strand does not gel. Yet James Diedrick may be right to suggest that 'the Royce Traynor plot serves as a master-trope for the theme of male malignity that suffuses the novel.'[8] Diedrick is responding to Robert Douglas-Fairhurst's very favourable and thoughtful review of *Yellow Dog*, and especially his observation that each of the novel's stories is motivated by the 'itch of vengeance', the circular reprisal 'that threatens to reverse personal and cultural development'.[9] The way in which that familiar story of masculinity might be refashioned in the post-9/11 moment deserves some attention.

Without question, the treatment of pornography, conceived as 'the obscenification of everyday life' (p. 335), is at the centre of this book and its depiction of civilization in crisis. The pornographer (Joseph Andrews) dispenses and receives extreme violence; Cora Susan, or 'Karla White', former porn star and now a producer, was raped by her father in childhood; and the users of pornography in the novel, such as Clint Smoker, are shown to be incapable of a functioning relationship. The blow to Xan Meo's head, from the extended hand of pornographer Andrews, clearly symbolizes how pornography can poison the male imagination: after the attack, he becomes sexually violent towards his wife, and predatory around his daughters, in an atavistic resurfacing of male aggression.

The attack on Xan, however, also symbolizes the now perennial fear of terrorism (invariably characterized as a 'Western' fear), and this dual symbolism points to a fundamental contradiction. Just as the pornographer's 'blow' to the male head sets off a train of sexual violence, and the seeds of social dissolution, so does Xan's desire for vengeance after the attack signify a more general political desire for justice/vengeance in response to terrorism, with a consequent loss of global stability: in this, there is a symbolic portrait of a civilization that is being undermined from within, while under attack from without, both threats unleashing a self-destructive violence. As a post-9/11 analysis, this is extraordinary, because pornography can be seen as the epitome of the permissiveness that Islamic extremists see as the great evil of the Western way of life. Read in one way, then, *Yellow Dog* shows Western civilization to be destroying itself in precisely the manner that its great global antagonist would expect.

Of course, neither this novel nor Amis's conception of the post-9/11 world is premised on a contest of equal antagonists. Indeed, since 2001 Amis has forged an uncompromising view that the form of militant Islamic extremism represented by Al-Qaeda is a form of distilled hatred. This 'Islamism' does not qualify as a worldview: 'Millennial Islamism is an ideology superimposed upon a religion – illusion upon illusion. It is not merely violent in tendency. Violence is all that is there.'[10] So, in tracing the contradictory and self-destructive forces of male sexuality abroad in Western society, he is implicitly expressing a notion of gender relations, and is exercising a form of rationality, neither of which would be feasible in an Islamist state, since 'the champions of militant Islam are, of course, misogynists, woman-haters; they are also misologists – haters of reason.'[11]

Amis's work – *Money* in particular – is sometimes felt to be too close to the 'junk' culture it criticizes; yet that strangely ambivalent position, in which dependence and ridicule are simultaneously apparent, is perhaps the only one available for a truly *rational* writer. And this is simply because there is no position outside of a culture from which its operations can be properly imagined and understood. This is the sense in which comedy (of the type written by Amis) and reason go together. Yet, as the finishing of *Yellow Dog* was Amis's *reply* to the Islamist attack on America, this particular conjunction of comedy and reason acquires a larger political significance than it would have had in earlier novels, since the very manner of writing tacitly announces a reply to millennial Islamism, and claims for itself a form of rationality which is alien to that ideology. From Amis's perspective, we are in a realm beyond the question of simple partisanship, here, since the work of the novelist cannot but align itself with the form of rationality that the new force of unreason, embodied in Islamism, seeks to extirpate. I will have more to say about this curiously bipolar world moment later in the chapter. First, I wish to attend to a characteristic feature of Amis's writing that lies at the other pole in the general/particular dichotomy: his trademark style, discernible in single descriptive sentences.

Amis's style may not always imply how a particular character 'felt about something'; but it invariably builds into a mood-setting that befits the characterization while also conveying the author's larger vision. One of the most incisive pieces of immediate post-9/11 commentary was embodied in the following detail, from Amis's article published on 18 September 2001: 'I have never seen a generically familiar object so transformed by effect. That second plane looked eagerly alive, and galvanized with malice, and wholly alien. For those thousands in the south tower, the second plane meant the end of everything. For us, its glint was the worldflash of the coming future.'[12] This typically acute observation records what many felt. The image of *that* plane is etched onto the mind of every person who has seen the footage, transforming the idea of 'plane' forever.[13]

However, if Amis was once generally held to be a pioneering stylist – the model for a generation of young (mostly male) novelists – later in his career, there has been far less unanimity about the quality of his descriptive writing. This is certainly evidenced in the reviews of *Yellow Dog*. Just one example will serve to make the point. For one reviewer, the following sentence was an example of Amis's descriptive brilliance: 'the contrails of the more distant aeroplanes were like incandescent spermatozoa, sent out to fertilize the universe' (p. 8).[14] In another article, however, it is this very sentence that is singled out as an illustration of bad writing in the book.[15] I note this arresting divergence of opinion not just because it illustrates the difficulty of evaluating Amis's worth; it also raises the possibility that his style is simultaneously good and bad – or, more accurately, arresting, because it is sometimes uncomfortable or embarrassing. The sentence in question here might seem, in isolation, a dressed-up adolescent fancy; yet in a novel haunted by the new significance of the aeroplane, and by various ideas of sex and death that are made to adhere to that context, we must recognize something acute behind the apparently obvious. Many of Amis's effects work in this way, pushing at something startling behind the obvious or the ugly.

Amis's association of ideas are denoted by the title, which links the unscrupulous and sensationalist 'yellow press' with an earlier form of political unreason: in the American South, in the nineteenth and early twentieth century, a Yellow Dog democrat was someone who, it was said, would vote for a yellow dog before voting for a Republican, so deep did resentments dating back to the Civil War run. Amis attached a broader context to the various social and political references that imply contempt for the 'yellow dog': in the round of interviews on the publication of *Yellow Dog*, Amis explains 'yellow' with reference to the post-9/11 climate, 'and the moral shift in the atmosphere. It's no longer a blue planet, or a grey planet, but a yellow planet.'[16]

If *Yellow Dog* is Amis's response to this jaundiced world, its fault-lines, arguably, are intended to reveal the limits of the novel in the face of these global changes. The design amounts to a conscious stretching of comedy to encompass a moment of global seriousness that Amis's formulation – for establishing reason through the comic vision – cannot fully encompass. The question is whether or not the prognosis for the novel is as grim as this implies. To get a sense of this, it is necessary to step back from the current historical moment, and to address a longer history of literary treatments of terrorism, in which the kind of limit identified by Amis is not uncommon; and so, perhaps, not specific to the twenty-first century.

In *Holy Terror*, Terry Eagleton points out that terrorism first emerged as a political idea with the French Revolution, but that 'in a broader sense of the word . . . terrorism is as old as humanity itself.' Much of his analysis – more 'metaphysical', he suggests, than conventional political accounts – has to do with how the Dionysian impulse becomes a death-drive in the world, as chaotic forces are unleashed upon the order of civilization.[17] For my purposes, it is the impact of terrorism upon the modern novel that is crucial, and Eagleton's literary readings embrace one novel which is germane, and to which I shall return: Conrad's *The Secret Agent*.

He also mentions in passing another unavoidable instance, Dostoevsky's *The Devils*, and this is an important test case for the problem that figures largely in post-9/11 novels: the extent to which the mind-set of the terrorist is unavailable or resistant to the subtle narrative teasing-out that we prize in the novel as the pre-eminent form of literary expression in the twenty-first century. The elusiveness of the terrorist's psyche implies an alien and resistant otherness that seems to mark the novel out as belonging to a very different camp. Are certain novelists in Britain and the US inevitably pushed, however marginally, towards the camp of Western liberal democracy and global capitalism, with the novel now disburdened, however slightly, of the relative autonomy that we have been wont to claim for it hitherto?

106

Twenty-first-century anxieties are put into perspective by reflecting on Dostoevsky – and the sense of *déjà vu* that reflection brings – for the significance of Dostoevsky for the modern European novel has surely to do with the way his unsettling plots chime with the experience of modernity, raising large and unresolvable questions about morality and belief. In *The Devils*, for example, Dostoevsky's local inspiration, in the nihilists of the 1860s, gives rise to a treatment of the tension between political terrorism and bourgeois values that exposes a host of anxieties contingent upon the 'progress' of the modern world. In one sense, the novel serves to demonize the revolutionary perspective. The devils or demons of the novel are those consuming ideas that drive the characters to desperate and wicked acts, as in the prosecution of terrorist activities in the pursuit of freedom. The 'sin', here, is a kind of free-floating human auto-nomy detached from ideas of rationality or explicability, a mysterious and essentially unknowable state of being. This mysterious autonomy is expressed most fully in the portrait of Stavrogin, a character whose mind is entirely unavailable to the reader.

Yet, if the amoral autonomy of the terrorist is not representable within the world of the novel, remaining a demonic other, there is also a sense in which this otherness reflects on the established bour-geois world. Indeed, a crucial aspect of Dostoevsky's *The Devils* is the *affinity* that is revealed between the revolutionaries and those who would uphold the social order, in terms of their demeanour and their values. As Peter Conradi has it, 'the posturing hysteria and airy futility of the governing class ... mirror the militant hysteria and fatuity of the nihilists.'[18] This is not to make a glib point about opposition, about how society has to imagine and expel its mirror image, and so begets its own nemesis. The question of affinity, which is an evolving aspect of Dostoevsky's vision here, suggests something richer and more complex in the way fiction imagines the collapse of the world that sustains it.

Eagleton's analysis traces one important 'reason why English literature, offspring of the longest-established middle-class nation in history, returns again and again to the secret complicity between the criminal and the capitalist': it is simply that 'the honest bourgeois detests the bohemian and the iconoclast ... partly because he has more in common with them than he cares to admit', a principle that also works in reverse: thus, Moll Flanders, though 'a thief and a whore, ... plies her trade as hard-headedly as any banker'; while Mr Merdle 'the master financier of Dickens's *Little Dorrit*, turns out to be a cheap crook.' In the same roll-call, we have Conrad's Verloc, 'both a small shopkeeper and an underground political *provocateur* responsible for the slaughter of his mentally defective stepson.' However, Eagleton shows how Conrad exposes the contradiction implicit in the terrorist act in *The Secret Agent*. Mr Vladimir, the architect of the terrorist plot, desires 'an act of destructive ferocity so absurd as to be incomprehensible'; yet the notion of a purely 'symbolic or expressive' act of terror, rather than one that is understood in 'instrumental' terms, is undermined by Vladimir's remarks about the Greenwich Observatory as a target that will hit at the 'sensibilities' of 'the middle classes': as Eagleton observes, 'Vladimir thus makes the point against his own intentions that political terror is not in fact sheerly purposeless.'[19]

For Eagleton, *The Secret Agent* is 'the first suicide-bomber novel of English literature', which makes it a seminal work in his analysis of suicide bombing as 'a supreme exercise of the will, which is part of what binds it to the civilization it opposes'. The emphasis placed by most of the revolutionary types in the novel on 'political action as a means to an end' is, observes Eagleton, 'a view which risks making them the mirror-images of their political opponents'. It is the Professor who appears to escape the contradiction, who desires a motiveless revolutionary act, and who, walking the streets of London with a bomb strapped to his body, 'has achieved a freedom which is at once empty and absolute'. The flaw with such a fantasy, as Eagleton eloquently observes, is that 'actions cannot be pure, because they have effects which are in principle incalculable'. The blowing to bits of the innocent Stevie underscores the grim lesson that 'matter cannot be annihilated'; from which it follows 'there can be no absolutely original future, since any imaginable future must be fashioned out of the tainted materials of the present.'

Eagleton then makes some arresting connections worthy of analysis. First, he suggests that the Professor is 'a parody of a modernist artist:

elitist, anti-bourgeois, beyond good and evil'. He then posits a line that connects the 'Professor's real adversary', which is 'the material world itself', with the tendency in Conrad's fiction for central events to be 'squinted at sideways rather than seen head-on': the killing of Verloc by his wife is one such instance, a decisive and desperate act of self-assertion, which, in its absence as a described event, reveals Conrad's affiliation with 'elitist modernist' art, thinks Eagleton: 'the indestructibility of the everyday, its stolid persistence in its own dull self-deluded being, is in one sense as repugnant to the novel as it is to the Professor.'

The horror of the deadly Professor is paralleled with that 'state authority' embodied in the devious Mr Vladimir, and for Eagleton this puts the novel in a complex position of contradictory complicity, given his characterization of Conrad as 'rabid opponent of political radicalism and a passionate devotee of social order'. The force of the irony here serves to link the chain of ideas: because the novel, in this reading, 'satirizes the commonplace petty-bourgeois world, while exploiting its very commonplaceness to discredit those out to devastate it', it stands, like the terrorist, in opposition to the materiality of social life.[20] It is a form of rarefied modernist elitism, from which a direct parallel can be drawn with the fantasy of terrorist purity, which, in turn, is paralleled in the operations of the state. The personal views of the author align him with one side in this dyad of terror, and bind his novel – through its very form – to the worldview it would repudiate.

It is worth remarking that this perspective, however valuable, denies the author a consciousness of the complicity that is central and obvious in the novel's own analysis, while implicitly staking out an autonomous vantage point of its own. Critics are apt to credit the more obvious self-consciousness of contemporary authors more willingly. However, in looking for a lesson in Conrad it is important to bear the specifics of his context in mind. Alex Houen, for example, reads the treatment of terrorism in *The Secret Agent* in relation to 'the problems that terrorist violence and anti-terrorist legislation presented for British liberalism at the time.' Thus, Mr Vladimir's plan to generate a political outrage reflects the dismay of other European states in the face of 'Britain's asylum policy', which, it was felt, 'simply helped terrorists': the symbolic outrage might force the government's hand, and 'elicit more stringent policing'.[21] This is a view that chimes with contemporary perspectives about Britain's traditional asylum policy, of course. In this view, *The Secret Agent* has its place in a longer modern problem still working itself out. The unwitting complicity Eagleton detects in Conrad's novel suggests a fault-line with an immediate contemporary resonance, the failure to establish a moral vantage point from which a valid or convincing judgement might emerge.

My reading of *Yellow Dog* reveals a similar yet more obviously conscious complicity, where the 'yellow' social and cultural world of Britain and the US is also the world repudiated in the ideology of Islamism. Amis makes the novel complicitous with this world, through its style and its preoccupations, in a deliberate and paradoxical gesture that aims to reclaim the ground of rationality. The gesture also serves, in the final analysis, to dismantle the West/Islam opposition by supplanting it with the opposing forces of reason/unreason, if one refuses to overlay the first opposition with the second.

The comparison with Conrad suggests that the threat terror poses to the world of the novel is not new, and may not require quite the dramatic formal splitting apart envisaged in Amis's anxious composition. One should remember, however, that the hyperbolic design is often crucial to Amis's effects. Moreover, it is the self-conscious exposure of complicity, revealed through the principle of reading partially 'with the grain', that defuses the anxiety and makes the aesthetic treatment of the political problem tenable.

A pre-9/11 novel that raises many similar issues, and which therefore embodies an informative point of comparison, is Philip Roth's *American Pastoral*, 'a Rothian elegy for the lost American Dream'.[22] The story of the high school sports star and wartime marine 'Swede' Levov, who marries the Miss New Jersey of 1949, and who successfully takes over his family's glove-making business, grafts successful cultural assimilation on to the career of commercial success: he is the Jew who becomes the stereotypical all-American hero, and who gets the Gentile girl, but who is faithful to his father's tradition of responsible capitalism, having crossed him just the once, in his choice of bride. The couple – he 'post-Jewish', she 'post-Catholic' in Levov's brother's view (p. 73) – seem to embody the postwar American optimism rooted in honest hard work, family values and cultural hybridity. When they set up their rural home in Old Rimrock, every plank of the postwar American idyll seems to be in place. The daughter Merry then emerges as the embodiment of chaos, bred from within: radicalized by the Vietnam War, she joins the group known as The Weathermen and, in 1968, plants a bomb in the Old Rimrock general store and post office, killing a local doctor.

It is 'the daughter who transports [Levov] out of the longed-for American pastoral and into everything that is its antithesis and its enemy, into the fury, the violence, and the desperation of the counterpastoral – into the indigenous American berserk' (p. 86). Yet these are the words of Nathan Zuckerman, Roth's narrator, who fashions the story of Levov, and whose role is crucial in the way we experience the novel. I will return to this issue. For now, it is important to note that the conceit of the book, in terms of how Swede Levov's story is grounded, is to accord external veracity to the outline given above, which is based on Zuckerman's own childhood memories of Levov, on two subsequent encounters with him in later life, and on the account of the brother, Jerry Levov, at the 45th high school reunion Zuckerman attends.

After 9/11, it is easy to appropriate earlier works like *American Pastoral*, and to make them speak to later deliberations on terror; and we should remember, as the story begins to take shape in Zuckerman's mind, he puts the issue of terror in a more precise postwar context, a particular point of 'historical transition' culminating in 'the sixties and . . . the disorder occasioned by the Vietnam War'. He is thinking, Zuckerman says, of 'families full of tolerance and kindly, well-intentioned liberal goodwill, and theirs were the kids who went on a rampage, or went to jail, or disappeared underground' (p. 88). Yet, in a developing new phase of terror – *American Pastoral* was published in 1997 – one can see Roth inviting a connection between the ideological turmoil and national crisis occasioned by Vietnam, and the emerging ideological stand-off that is later etched starkly on American consciousness in 2001.

Other elements in the book all serve to embellish the grand theme, the collapse of the American pastoral in a broader and ongoing postwar perspective. The treatment of the glove-making business is crucial, since the family company symbolizes the world of capital accumulation that Merry rejects. The impression one is left with, finally, arises not from the fanaticism of Lou Levov, but, rather from nostalgic reverence for the erstwhile skill of the glove-maker, which comes over in several extended passages which articulate – and implicitly celebrate – this craft associated with successive generations of immigrant workers. There is a sense of ownership in the detail of the craftsmanship, so that manufacturing comes to be associated in the reader's mind (as in the mind of Swede Levov) with a particular community.[23]

In short, the treatment of the Newark Maid glove company leads us away from insular fanaticism, and towards the opposing value of benign, paternal industrialism; of, that is to say, 'bourgeois virtues that are easier to sneer at than to replicate'.[24] If the novel is a 'bourgeois' art form, it does not usually announce its values so clearly as this. Pertinent to this discussion is that aspect of a liberal sensibility that unites novelists and novel readers, and which determines the business of the novelist: the interest in the components of personality.

From the perspective of any reader in admiration of sophisticated self-consciousness, this is where Roth's novel is particularly fascinating, because Merry, the combatant of the bourgeois world, is also the character lacking in personality, and so the character who is most resistant to the novelist's imagination. In the meeting Zuckerman conjures between Levov and Merry, she has swapped one extreme ideology for another, having abandoned revolutionary violence for an ultimate form of pacifism. Explaining her conversion to Jainism – the mystical Indian religion based on the sanctity of life – Merry says: 'I am bound to harm no living being, neither man, nor animal, nor plant' (p. 243). The ultimate goal of this religion, the perfection of its followers, is self-starvation. This brings to mind the haunting image of the Buddhist monks setting fire to themselves, in 1962 or 1963 'before the war in Vietnam had begun in earnest', which Levov offers as a formative moment in Merry's childhood, on the way to becoming a terrorist (pp. 153–4).

I will leave aside, for a moment, the fact that both episodes are Zuckerman's fabrication, and the pattern of development they imply is his notion. What is interesting is the difficulty the writer has in embracing fanaticism within the discourse of the novel. The significance of this has been well observed by Mark Shechner, who asks, pointedly: 'How does the novelist bring to life someone who has taken the oath to deny all the superfluous debris of the middle-class life that goes into the formation of personality?' And he wonders if 'personality – self-questioning, the interior monologue, the interior dialogue, the quirky and elaborate accretions of manners and habits, memories and ideas' – might not be 'an impediment to . . . "revolutionary praxis"'.[25]

Yet Roth's emphasis is the *response* to extremism, rather than extremism *per se*. Zuckerman presents Swede Levov as experiencing the classic liberal dilemma of inaction, which is brought into focus for him by his failure to respond effectively to the extreme positions taken by his daughter: 'No, he wasn't a Jain, thought the Swede, but he might as well have been – he was just as pathetically and naively non-violent. The idiocy of the uprightness of the goals he had set' (p. 252). Later, Zuckerman has Levov's brother Jerry berate him in still harsher terms, fraternal resentment merely exaggerating the charges that the novel lays at the door of all good Americans: 'You're the one who always comes off looking good. And look where it's got you. Refusing to give offense. Blaming yourself. Tolerant respect for every position. Sure, it's "liberal" – I know, a liberal father. But what does that mean? What is at the *center* of it? Always holding things together. And look where the fuck it's got you!' (p. 279).

Roth skilfully generates tension through Levov's Hamletesque angst about action, and fosters an expectation that Levov will eventually throw off, dramatically, his liberal garb as the provocation builds; but such a cathartic conclusion is pointedly avoided. Along the way, however, Levov shows signs of defiant anger. Frank Kermode has

113

written perceptively of Roth's outrageousness as a necessary feature of his novels – 'if nobody feels outraged the whole strategy has failed'[26] – and Zuckerman has Levov produce such a moment in his perception of his festering fugitive daughter, after becoming a Jain, when he is still wrestling with his disbelief about Merry as the Rimrock bomber:

> Her foulness had reached him. She is disgusting. His daughter is a human mess stinking of human waste. Her smell is the smell of everything organic breaking down. It is the smell of no coherence. It is the smell of all she's become. She could do it, and she did do it, and this reverence for life is the final obscenity. (p. 265)

Then, as he cries out his elemental question '*Who are you!*', a 'bitter, acidic stream' of 'gastric secretions' is 'spewed with his words onto her face' (pp. 265–6). Levov's transgression, having invaded his daughter's space to tear off her veil, is compounded by the final loss of faith in the idea of her innocence, the rejection of her identity, the disgust, the vomit. It is the final undoing of the proper liberal, father-daughter relationship that is shocking, most especially because Levov's own identity is founded upon such relationships.

More purposively, Levov shows signs of making judgements about others in these final pages, and certainly of recognizing that his inability to read people has been his great failing: 'he had failed to see into his daughter, failed to see into his wife, failed to see into his one and only mistress – probably had never even begun to see into himself. What was *he*, stripped of all the signs he flashed?' (pp. 409–10). In this light, Levov's inclination to enact violent retribution upon Bill Orcutt, having discovered the affair between Orcutt and his wife, seems more than the jealousy of the cuckolded husband. It is based upon a new inclination to judge Orcutt: 'Yes, something is wrong with this guy, there always was, and the Swede had known it all along' (p. 381).

Yet all of this we take to be Zuckerman's invention. Building upon the outline of Swede Levov's tragedy, he creates explanations which make sense of his own view of American decline, and also his own concerns as a writer. Indeed, the business of making judgements about others is established early on as a seminal topic for Zuckerman, who concludes that 'getting people right is not what living is all about anyway. It's getting them wrong that is living, getting them wrong and wrong and wrong and then, on careful reconsideration, getting them wrong again. That's how we know we're alive: we're wrong' (p. 35). Just before this there is an implication that writers have a privileged insight into the interior life; but, at the same time, their 'word people' are disconnected from 'the real people that we mangle' in common experience. This principle is dramatized within the novel in the comparison we seem to be invited to make between Zuckerman's imagined Levov, brought to the brink of a final and terminal collapse in 1973, and the Levov Zuckerman has actually met, in 1985 and again in 1995, who has married again and raised three boys with the help of a 'good-looking blonde' wife, who deferred her own career until the boys were all at school (p. 23): Levov, it seems, has had a second, successful attempt to produce the perfect all-American family.

If, however, the tragic denouement that seems to be building is not delivered, there is still an emphasis on the damaging gap between appearance and reality. Swede Levov's new family has all the trappings of American success, which does not distinguish it from his previous family. The career of the second wife – advertising manager for a weekly paper – is pointedly associated with the superficial, the meretricious. When he meets Levov at a restaurant, Zuckerman is troubled by the surface assurance of the man, at the time deciding 'this guy is the embodiment of nothing' (p. 39). We discover, of course, that he was already dying of the cancer that claims him just two months later (p. 64).

The real tragedy, then, has to do with the inability to penetrate the surface, to deal with that which lurks beneath. Levov and the other characters at the vividly imagined dinner party at the end of the novel do not have the complexity to warrant a truly literary tragic ending; but that is their real tragedy. As a consequence, the final scene descends into farce. As Levov is provoked, seemingly beyond endurance, and brought to the brink of a murderous outburst, he remains constrained by the etiquette of the occasion (despite a thunderous exchange with his former mistress Sheila Salzman): 'his daughter was an insane murderer hiding on the floor of a room in Newark, his wife had a lover who dry-humped her over the sink in their family kitchen, his ex-mistress had knowingly brought disaster upon his house, and he was trying to propitiate his father with on-the-one-hand-this and on-the-other-hand-that' (p. 358).

Yet Levov is made to imagine a properly tragic conclusion to the scene (and to the novel), when he hears his father screaming: he imagines Merry has arrived and has informed her grandfather (as she has informed her father) that she has killed *four* people in total, thus destroying the old man with the weak heart (pp. 419–21). In fact, the drunken Mrs Orcutt has attempted, unsuccessfully, to stab the old man – who has been feeding her, in the hope of sobering her up – in the eye, with her fork. Not the resounding conclusion to the family tragedy, but rather a bathetic moment that 'parodies the Jewish focus on eating to excess and their view that Christians drink to excess'.[27] That this dinner party should descend into an act of cross-faith petty violence plainly casts doubt on the idea of 'the neutral, dereligionized ground of Thanksgiving' as 'the American pastoral par excellence' (p. 402). Those gathered at the dinner party have some notion that they are struggling to establish their social values; but their positions are undermined by their various duplicities and betrayals.

There is, however, something theoretical about this closing scene. We know Levov later remarries, and has a second attempt at the American Pastoral, so the device of making the novel conclude at the key low point for Levov of 1973 – and making his tragedy descend bathetically into farce – is pointedly artificial. It is Zuckerman's (and Roth's) device, a device that sets up the closing rhetorical questions, where the authorial voice merges with the narrator's: 'And what is wrong with their life? What on earth is less reprehensible than the life of the Levovs?' (p. 423). Here the novel reveals its hand, as being confined by a form of discourse necessarily geared to the treatment of liberal personality or identity. It is worth remembering that such treatment invariably involves bringing that identity to a point of crisis, so Roth is exposing a crucial capacity of the novel in the direct address in these closing sentences. This is the kind of crisis that is then given a particular intensity in the post-9/11 novel, but which is thoroughly anticipated by Roth.

In view of its literary antecedents, John Updike's *Terrorist* (2006) follows a familiar pattern, as an apparent exercise in trying to understand the mind-set of Islamic extremism. The plot is reduced to bare outlines, and there are implausible coincidences to speed us through the requisite settings for the enlistment of 18-year-old New Jersey boy, Ahmad Ashmawy Molloy, half-Irish, half-Egyptian, as an Al-Qaeda terrorist, driving a van packed with explosives to detonate in the Lincoln Tunnel.

The novel was not well received, though some reviewers were prepared to see something worthy in the presentation of Ahmad, without feeling Updike had offered any great insight. Stephen Abell, for instance, reads Ahmad as a 'young man righteously repelled by the uncivilized world and wrongly manipulated as a result.' Yet he still sees this as 'an unnaturally reductive portrait' because 'the relentlessness of Ahmad's piety is not contextualized'. He stands 'for nothing other than his religion', and so 'is no more than a Muslim Metonymy'.[28]

Trying hard to get on Updike's wavelength, Jem Poster recognized he was 'urging us towards a deeper understanding of Islamic fundamentalism'.[29] But neither of these appraisals ascribes much literary merit to the novel: it is either a false projection, or an earnest (and urgent) effort of social understanding. In fact, the novel's literary quality – in the sense that I am working with 'literariness' in this chapter, as a form of self-conscious anxiety that is revealing, in the face of terror – emerges in the space between the two views, the condemnation or the appreciation of trying to 'understand' a character like Ahmad.

Indeed, the complaint that Updike does not fully explain someone like Ahmad is curious when you think about the confused context into which the book emerges. Stephen Amidon thinks Ahmad implausible, since he is depicted in part as 'a fairly typical alienated American teenager', but otherwise 'he thinks and talks like the brainwashed product of some Karachi madrassa'. As a consequence, thinks Amidon, Updike is unable 'to show how these two personali- ties – the rebellious American kid and the fundamentalist soldier of Islam – feed off one another.'[30]

It would, indeed, be a marvellous document that might show how these two personalities feed off one another; and one hopes that community groups and government working parties, in Britain and the US, will continue the monumental and complex task of addressing this matter. But it is not the work of the novelist. Indeed, Updike is at pains to establish that Ahmad is not of a recognizable community, and so is inscrutable in relation to available social norms: he is dismissive of ordinary Muslims in city neighbourhoods, 'who are enrolled in Islam as a lazy matter of ethnic identity'. Ahmad has a 'pride of isolation and willed identity' that he feels to be 'threatened' by these masses (p. 177).

He has a parallel, however, in 63-year-old careers guidance counsellor Jack Levy, the lapsed Jew whose view of contemporary American society is sometimes akin to Ahmad's. He has a perception of the young sliding 'into the fatal morass of the world – its dwindling resources, its disappearing freedoms, its merciless advertisements geared to a preposterous popular culture of eternal music and beer and impossibly thin and fit young females' (p. 23). This is not so very different from Ahmad's perception of the 'infidels' who surround him, 'slaves to images, false ones of happiness and affluence' (p. 4). The key difference, of course, is that Jack displays concern for the young, imagining himself 'shouting out' to them, whereas Ahmad has been conditioned to see the 'infidels' as figures of hatred, worthy of destruction.

Updike is not interested in exploring that difference; but, rather, in constructing a plot that will efface it. Here we must consider Updike's celebrated style, and how it is put to service in *Terrorist*. For most reviewers, his arresting descriptive work seems no more than a sideshow in relation to the book's urgent central theme, a kind of helpless reversion to type that is inadequate to the task at hand.[31]

Yet this apparent 'inadequacy' is what Updike makes us focus on. Jack Levy's perspective is, at times, infused with an Updikean sensuality – most obviously in his sexual appraisal of Ahmad's mother Terry during their affair; but there is a comparable propensity in Ahmad, which culminates in his revelation in the Lincoln Tunnel, as he is on the point of detonating his explosives: the pattern of the tiles on the wall and ceiling 'explodes outward in Ahmad's mind's eye in the gigantic fiat of Creation, one concentric wave after another, each pushing the other farther and farther out from the initial point of nothingness' (p. 306). For Ahmad, the revelation is filtered through a religious consciousness; but it is the delight in the perception of reality that produces it. Updike gives us, pointedly, an explosion of conscious awareness as the revelation that prevents the other kind of explosion; and this spontaneous delight in life manifests itself in the smile Ahmad gives to the children in the car in front, suddenly reprieved from sudden death (p. 307).

It is not a conversion; but the delight in the observation of things is presented as that which must stop the terrorist in his tracks, and as our hope of finding common ground, across cultural differences. Such sensory perception is also, of course, the most celebrated achievement of Updike as novelist so, tacitly, a rather grand claim is being made for the role of the novel. How much significance are we prepared to attach to that sensory eye for detail, the Updikean gift for arresting descriptions of diurnal reality? Updike's point is to emphasize the frailty of the novelist's tools, paralleled in the frailty of Jack Levy/levee as a defence against the terrorist attack. If the levee holding back extremism comprises ageing and disillusioned people like Levy, then Updike is presumably signalling how easily it might break; but the work of the novelist is tied in to this task of finding common ground, in a gesture that is paradoxically humble and grandiose at the same time.

If it is right that '*Terrorist* does not presume to explain Ahmad so much as try to get to know him', Updike is trying to make the terrorist mind less alien, without being able to penetrate it.[32] There is no 'conversion' for Ahmad away from his Islamist tendencies, but a kind of enforced redemption through the discovery of consciousness and sensory perception as a necessary common ground. Martin Amis makes a parallel, though more audacious, attempt to imagine the terrorist mind-set in his short story 'The Last Days of Muhammad Atta', which fictionalizes Atta's thought processes on 9/11. It is a very different piece of fiction; but one which, finally, 'faces down' the terrorist in the same way that Updike's *Terrorist* does.

The impetus of Amis's story is to uncover the psychosis that drives Islamism. In the case of Atta, it is not religion that is the appeal so much as an encoded form of misogynistic violence: 'if you took away all the rubbish about faith, then fundamentalism suited his character, and with an almost sinister precision. For example, the attitude to women: the blend of extreme hostility and extreme wariness he found highly congenial.' Amis propounds a familiar idea to explain the attraction of *jihad* to young men: the channelling of the repressed sexual urge through an ideology combining 'ferocity and rectitude'. This may be convincing to some; but it is clearly a form of armchair psychoanalysis that serves to ridicule the terrorist in base terms: of the uptight Atta, we read: 'he had not moved his bowels since May.'[33] It would normally be impossible to complain about such rudimentary character portraits in a piece by Amis, since this is the kind of material from which his comic worlds are built. This story, however, is a fictional exercise to get inside the mind of Atta, and it makes a tacit claim for a form of verisimilitude that is uncharacteristic of his work.

Pursuing the principle of verisimilitude the story demands, its more challenging aspect is located in the attempt to engage the suicide bombers' cult of death. In an important essay, Amis points out that this is the great difficulty: 'suicide-mass murder is astonishingly alien, so alien, in fact, that Western opinion has been unable to formulate a rational response to it. A rational response would be something like an unvarying factory siren of unanimous disgust.' In this essay, Amis emphasizes this sense of alienation, and resorts to a coinage to convey the utter abomination of this new form of 'maximum malevolence', which is not terrorism but 'horrorism'.[34]

In the story, there is an attempt to articulate the attraction of mass killing – this manifestation of horrorism – in terms of power. The 'core reason' for the attacks is alluded to throughout, but not explained until the final page, where killing emerges as a fantasy of 'divine delight'. In the conclusion of the story, however, Amis undermines this fantasy through a compelling emphasis on materiality. Here, Amis interrogates the idea of instant death, suggesting – in the manner of Tobias Wolff in his extraordinary story, 'Bullet in the Brain' – that brain time, determined by lightning flashes of consciousness, is (paradoxically) much slower than the idea of instant death implies. So, for Atta, 'by the time the last second arrived, the first second seemed as far away as childhood.' This is the lesson for Atta, that it is not death, but the conscious experience of material life that is the only possible human realm:

> The physical torment – a panic attack in every nerve, a riot of the atoms – merely italicized the last shinings of his brain. They weren't thoughts; they were more like a series of unignorable conclusions, imposed from without.... How very gravely he had underestimated life. His own he had hated and wished away; but see how long it was taking to absent itself – and with what helpless grief was he watching it go, imperturbable in its beauty and its power. Even as his flesh fried and his blood boiled, there was life, kissing its fingertips. Then it echoed out, and ended.[35]

Where Updike's terrorist Ahmad experiences an internal explosion of conscious awareness about the primacy of lived experience (filtered through religious interpretation), Amis proposes that the experience of death, for the mass-suicide bomber Atta, obliges him to re-evaluate life.

Amis ends his article on Millennial Islamism by appealing for a kind of quasi-spiritual rationality: 'opposition to religion already occupies the high ground, intellectually and, morally. People of independent mind should now start to claim the spiritual high ground, too.' A lengthy quotation from Conrad's 'Author's Note' (1920) to *The Shadow-Line* indicates what he has in mind: he is inspired by Conrad's stress on 'the world of the living', with its 'marvels and mysteries acting upon our emotions and intelligence in ways so inexplicable that it would almost justify the conception of life as an enchanted state.' By contrast, for Conrad, 'the mere supernatural ... is but a manufactured article', and so 'a desecration of our tenderest memories, an outrage on our dignity.'[36]

121

The appeal to Conrad in this context seems lame; partly because of Conrad's own fascinating and ambivalent struggle to address the psyche of the terrorist, but also because this appeal reveals a cyclical dilemma that cannot bring things to a head in the way that Amis's article seeks to do. Updike's comparable (but lower key) appeal to the novelist's art of description is also lame, but suggestive of a kind of creative continuity that is more inclined to sidestep the great ideological standoff that Islamism is eager to foist upon the world, between Islam and capitalist democracy. Amis's short story and essay both seem eager to enter the lists, something his novel *Yellow Dog* avoids.[37]

Refusing to fuel the confrontation now seems an urgent task for novelists and cultural commentators alike; and, in this respect, it seems important for us to repudiate the notion that the novel is a 'Western' form. A novel written intriguingly on the horns of this dilemma is Ian McEwan's *Saturday* (2005).

To contextualize McEwan's approach to *Saturday*, it is worth briefly retracing his attempts to grapple with the political and moral significance of the attack on America, beginning with his immediate responses. Looking back, McEwan's comments seem anodyne, a kind of temporary soothing balm. Even so, he did try and establish the moral high ground. This is most apparent in his front-page article for the *Guardian*, where he appears as a kind of global moralist, asserting a transcendent form of humanism. In this moving article, he expresses a horrified response to the four days of news about the attack. In particular, he focuses on those haunting final mobile phone calls made by those trapped in the Twin Towers: 'I love you . . . is what they were all saying.' These words, he writes, 'compel us to imagine ourselves into that moment. What would we say? Now we know.'

His evocation of 'empathy' and 'compassion' is also made to do work on the side of goodness in an elemental tussle. He thinks himself into the situation of a doomed passenger, in a demonstration of the link between imaginative projection and compassion, as a prelude to his central argument that the terrorists displayed 'a failure of the imagination'. The ability to imagine 'what it is like to be someone other than yourself is at the core of our humanity', he says, and 'the beginning of morality.'[38]

What is it, exactly, that McEwan is holding up in defiance of the terrorist? The rhetorical force of the article adapts a recognizable Christian ethic – service to others as a way of defeating wickedness – in order to hint at the important place occupied by the novelist in the process of moral thinking. That demonstration of imaginative projection, the basic ingredient of fiction writing, appears tacitly to justify the editorial decision to turn to a novelist for a judgement that will stand. Yet readers of McEwan were instantly presented with a paradox: they turned to *Atonement* (published in September 2001) and found a complex novel that is uncertain about the moral dimension of the novelist's imaginative projection.

McEwan's instant response to 9/11, published three days earlier, was a little different. Here he confesses to surfing TV news channels – rather as Perowne is described doing in *Saturday*, but 'hungrily, ghoulishly'. He wonders if the plotters 'were ... watching with us now, equally hungry to know the worst?' He goes on: 'the thought covered me in shame.'[39] There is something richer in this immediate response than there is in the piece about imaginative projection, with its implicit championing of a 'Western' cultural norm. McEwan's ambivalence about the author's position points to a certain complicity: the global media village connects the terrorist and the average viewer, producing a shared appetite for catastrophe. A generalized shame must flow from this, making a moral vantage point hard to establish.

In some respects, however, *Saturday* appears to be explicitly partisan in the new bipolar world. John Banville was dismayed by this, finding the novel to be 'self-satisfied', characterized by 'arrogance', and well received by Western readers who are reassured at a time when they are shaken in their sense of themselves and their culture.[40] More explicitly than the other novels discussed in this chapter, perhaps, *Saturday* is aligned with 'universal values' rooted in the principles of capitalist democracy. Yet the focus on 'Western' scientific discovery is used both to justify the notion of universality, and to put it in a broader historical and human perspective.

There is, however, a consonance between *Saturday* and the contemporaneous public mood that served to restrict its immediate impact, suggesting a straightforward allegorical strand that drives the suspense: the threat to the security of the Perownes parallels the broader insecurity of the West in the face of Islamic extremism, and in respect of those states seeking to foment anti-Western sentiment. To the extent that *Saturday* is an allegorical thriller, it follows a process of demonization conducted from a Western perspective, most especially in the parallel between Baxter and Saddam Hussein. In time, however, Baxter will surely become a figure for the terroristic other more generally.

Yet the novel is also partly anchored to the particular context through Perowne, who is a champion in a late phase of the machine age, in a novel that openly celebrates the technological enhancements of domestic life, as well as those that facilitate surgery; and in all of this, there is an undeveloped contradiction. The culture of Western scientific advancement, and technological comfort – the world of Perowne, and the culture of which *Saturday* is (necessarily) a part – is also the culture currently most to blame for global environmental degradation. This, of course, is the culture that is identified as the enemy by Islamic militants, though not out of concern for the environment.

If there is something brittle in the novel's topicality, the problem is partly eschewed by its other resonances. Indeed, the 'two cultures' debate displaces the post-9/11 Iraq war context and assumes central significance – though without finally permitting us to forget that context. There is a substantial and intriguing area of common ground between art and science, which hinges on Perowne's profession, and the advances in neurosurgery that McEwan explores through him. If advancing understanding of the brain is the occasion for a new form of wonder, McEwan speculates on how the novel might respond to this evolving discipline, with huge ramifications for our understanding of consciousness.

In his reverence for consciousness, Perowne is very close to McEwan who, in an article on science and belief, stated: 'what I believe but cannot prove is that no part of my consciousness will survive my death.' While acknowledging that 'many will take this premise as a given', McEwan points out that 'it divides the world crucially', separating the rationalists from those who have done great damage by virtue of the conviction 'that there is a life, a better, more important life, elsewhere'. The premise leads McEwan to the worldview enshrined in *Saturday*: 'that this span is brief, that consciousness is an accidental gift of blind processes, makes our existence all the more precious and our responsibilities for it all the more profound.'[41]

We appear to be back, then, to the divided post-9/11 world, and a novel that, despite its longer historical resonances, is partly constructed to fight the great damage done by those who believe in 'a better, more important life, elsewhere'. McEwan's reverence of consciousness faces down the delusions of the mass-suicide bomber. Yet this reverence also faces down the Christian fundamentalist, and perhaps more directly. What might finally taint the novel as a 'Western' product is its enthusiasm for scientific advances pioneered in the First World; but we should get used to challenging the idea that you cannot write from a privileged position without being 'partisan', since the alternative is silence. Scientific discoveries, of course, become more generally applicable over time. Neither is the appropriation of science in the name of capital an inherent feature of the process of discovery. The idealistic humanism of *Saturday*, rooted in this appreciation of disinterested science, may become more apparent as the context of the Iraq war recedes.

This is the aspect of *Saturday* that reveals it to aspire beyond the impasse reached by Conrad, Dostoevsky and Roth on account of the inability to *know* the mind that perpetrates unreasoned violence. *Saturday* gestures beyond this impasse, but this is something of an illusion: medical science can explain Baxter, but the texture of the novel does not embrace or imitate such a consciousness. Yet the other aspect of the Perowne/Baxter connection is to resist the idea of the self/other double, and the theme of complicity. If it is the genetic lottery, merely, that distinguishes Perowne from Baxter (rather than malign social engineering), Perowne still has the professional nous to recognize and respond to that distinction. This puts him in a position of moral responsibility, with a duty of care enacted in the decision to operate on Baxter and save his life.

Saturday, therefore, aspires to *encompass* and *understand* the alien, violent mind. The gesture is incomplete, and for some readers unconvincing; but McEwan is feeling his way beyond the central dilemma that haunts the post-9/11 novel in the hands of other prominent writers in Britain and the US, who seem bound to rehearse a very particularized sense of complicity that obstructs their global or cosmopolitan impulses. The extent to which these impulses are also obscured in academic literary criticism is a central preoccupation in the next chapter.

5

Global Futures: Novelists, Critics, Citizens

A main concern of this book has been to locate topics that should be of equal concern to novelists, critics and readers, with the aim of helping to reorientate academic literary criticism and theory. This is not, however, to propose a dramatic sea-change, a resurrection of the practice in which the literary critic presumes to pronounce with singular authority on the health of the culture. Yet there are crucial cultural and political issues in relation to which the modern-day literary critic or theorist should have a voice.

Novelists have been particularly sharp in questioning the currency and relevance of the work done by academics in literary studies. In *American Pastoral*, Roth creates the caricature of Marcia Umanoff, 'a literature professor in New York', and 'a militant nonconformist of staggering self-certainty much given to sarcasm and calculatedly apocalyptic pronouncements designed to bring discomfort to the lords of the earth' (p. 339). Her view – 'without transgression there isn't very much knowledge, is there?' (p. 360) – contrasts with the anxieties of the other characters at the dinner party at the end of Roth's novel, where 'wondering' and 'worrying where the limit is' characterizes the general mood (p. 365). Against this shared angst, Umanoff stands as an agent of unfettered transgression:

She began to laugh at their obtuseness to the flimsiness of the whole contraption, to laugh and laugh and laugh at them all, pillars of

127

a society that, much to her delight, was going rapidly under – to laugh and to relish, as some people, historically, always seem to do, how far the rampant disorder had spread, enjoying enormously the assailability, the frailty, the enfeeblement of supposedly robust things. (p. 423)

The effect of this, in the context of a novel haunted by how a terrorist act 'bred from within' blows apart the American Pastoral, is to associate the attitude of the literature professor with the psychology of the terrorist: both are amoral, both delight in the collapse of the existing social order. The automatic response of the academic in literary studies may be to dismiss the caricature of Marcia Umanoff as an example of anti-theory hyperbole. However, I do not think that such a portrayal, in a major work by America's leading novelist, can be treated so lightly. The theorist may not be the agent of social collapse; but we should, perhaps, reflect on how theoretical ideas sometimes lend themselves to simplification and misappropriation. (It is certainly true, for example, that student essays in which 'transgression' figures as an abstract concept, deemed to be wholly benign, have been common in recent years.)

In *The Human Stain* (2000), a sustained attack on political correctness, Roth picks up the connection between literary theory and personal delusion in the portrayal of another female academic, the French intellectual Delphine Roux.[1] Her campaign against Coleman Silk, the Dean who had appointed her to the intellectual backwater of Athena that she so despises, is rooted in her repudiation of his humanism and her perception of his misogyny; and it is prosecuted, initially, by her willingness to support the false charge of racism against him. All along, however, she has been suppressing the realization that she is deeply attracted to Silk – indeed, that he is her ideal man (p. 274).[2]

This personal delusion leads Roux to despicable acts, helping to destroy the reputation of Silk while he is alive, and encouraging her to frame him for a break-in on the night of his death. Through the creation of Roux, Roth rages against a society caught up in a new, insidious form of McCarthyism, the self-righteousness of ideological assertion parading as justice, and which brooks no dissent. In one

128

telling scene, Silk and Roux clash over the teaching of Euripides. Roux suggests that Silk should take into account the feminist perspective of his students, rather than pursuing his own 'purely disinterested literary perspective' (p. 191). His response is arrogant, yet telling: 'providing the most naive of readers with a feminist perspective on Euripides is one of the best ways you could devise to close down their thinking before it's even had a chance to begin to demolish a single one of their brainless "likes"'' (p. 192).

Roth's simple point – though, of course, he loads the dice in making it – is that the educator takes responsibility for the intellectual development of his or her students by extending their current thinking rather than by pandering to it. Beyond this, however, he is resisting the notion that a 'perspective' from which to teach literature should be predetermined. And as in literary appreciation, so in life: Roux sends the retired, widowed Silk a poison-pen letter when she discovers he is having an affair with Faunia Farley, an illiterate 34-year-old cleaning lady, having settled the matter in her own mind that Silk has found 'a misogynist's heart's desire' (p. 194). The poison-pen letter reads: 'Everyone knows you're sexually exploiting an abused, illiterate woman half your age' (p. 38). Roth is concerned to show how the certitude born of ideological conviction is a form of oppressive zealotry. It is this tendency to judge others that provokes Zuckerman's reflection: 'what underlies the anarchy of the train of events, the uncertainties, the mishaps, the disunity, the shocking irregularities that define human affairs? *Nobody* knows, Professor Roux' (p. 209). Zuckerman's own imaging of the erotic charge between Coleman Silk and Faunia Farley is very different: 'everything painful congealed into passion' (p. 203). In the extraordinary scene where Faunia dances for Coleman, she claims to be teaching him, as 'the formal transfer of power begins' (pp. 227–9).

At one point, Zuckerman has Silk consider the language of narratology to be a barrier for Roux, a way of allowing her 'to hide from the human dimension of her experience behind these words' (p. 190). Later, Zuckerman characterizes her as not having 'that much conviction about all the so-called discourse she picked up in Paris and New Haven', since 'it was always difficult for her to deal with literature through literary theory'. For Roux, 'there could be such a gigantic gap between what she liked and what she was supposed to admire – between how she was supposed to speak about what she was supposed to admire and how she spoke to herself about the writers she treasured' (pp. 266–7).

Roth presents literary theory as not just a cynical form of professional validation, but as a force for conformity that diminishes the literary, and, by extension, a force that diminishes the human experience. Of course, Roux's self-destructive conformity is paralleled in Silk's great secret: the suppression of his ethnicity in order to pass himself off as a white man, and succeed in his ambitions. In a novel that is concerned with the broader malaise of postwar America – set in the summer of the Bill Clinton/Monica Lewinsky affair, and a mood of prurient and hypocritical public condemnation – Roth is laying a significant charge at the door of literary theory, and the part he feels it to be playing in the spread of a wider social anomie. Coetzee's brittle feminist Faroodia Rasool, forcing the hand of the disciplinary committee in *Disgrace* (1999), is of a piece with Delphine Roux. Some academics will bridle at these caricatures. Some will be concerned by the gender issues they raise; but they remain influential portrayals that chime with a broader public perception of the narrowness of academia, a perception that must be acknowledged.

In relation to this topic, the new climate of terror produced a defining moment. On 4 October 2001, the *London Review of Books* published a symposium of responses to 9/11 written by prominent academics (and also past *LRB* contributors). It sparked a furore in the letters page, with a number of American readers – most notably Marjorie Perloff, whose response provoked a further controversy – feeling that the paper had published a series of Eurocentric attacks on the US, epitomized in Mary Beard's suggestion that 'many people openly or privately think' that 'the United States had it coming'.[3] Perloff led the way for a number of American readers who angrily cancelled their subscriptions.[4] An interesting divide was, indeed, opened up by the symposium and the subsequent correspondence, but it was not the dichotomy of the American versus the European perspective: as Denis McQuail pointed out a few weeks later, there were more contributors to the symposium based in the US than in Europe.[5] The divide that was glimpsed was a political one, based on the intellectual affiliation of the respective critics.

Most of the contributors wrote in the humane terms that were appropriate to the aftermath of 9/11, even while they were criticizing the Bush administration. Thus Terry Eagleton wrote of the 'moral obscenity wreaked' on the US, even while anticipating the retributive response that would cause it to 'squander' its briefly held 'moral advantage'; Edward Said placed emphasis on the backlash suffered by 'the seven million Muslim Americans', but acknowledged 'the understandable fear and anger that seem widespread all over the country'; and Michael Wood, who pointed out that 'many Americans are concerned about the role American policies have played in the creation of the climate which made the attacks possible' – even though 'no one is saying this publicly' – registered his main response through the image of the individuals choosing to throw themselves out of the Twin Towers, rather than face the horror within: 'falling from an immense height is the nightmare of many of us, and the thought of choosing this death, of seeing and knowing and refusing a worse death, is surely beyond nightmare.'[6] (As we shall see, it is the image of the falling man in particular that has imprinted itself on the consciousness of some leading American novelists.)

Typically, then, the symposiasts were humane, even while they were analytical, their critique of US policy invariably tempered by an empathic response to the suffering – or, one might say, the intellectualizing was conditioned by the spectacle of terror. Not so Fredric Jameson, who wrote, à la Baudrillard, that 'the event in question, as history, is incomplete and one can even say that it has not yet fully happened'. He condemned the 'nauseating media reception' for its 'cheap pathos', and, pointing out that 'the Americans created bin Laden during the Cold War', he concluded that the attack on America – or, rather, 'the "events" we imagine to have taken place on a single day in September' – constituted 'a textbook example of dialectical reversal'.[7] In refusing to temper his words in the way that Eagleton and Said did, Jameson's obstinacy revealed the unresponsiveness of a certain kind of poststructuralist thinking, in this

131

case a developed form of Western Marxism that, bizarrely, seemed impervious to its context.[8] The problem was not simply the feeling that, even if Jameson was partially right, he should not be saying these things, not now. It went further: the unnuanced and insensitive analysis seemed robotic, divorced from the life actually lived. And this raised a further spectre: was this indicative, more generally, of a kind of criticism, rooted in textuality and divorced from reality, that required adherence to certain incontrovertible analytical 'rules', rules that could be revealed as ethically bankrupt in the face of extreme external pressure?

More worryingly, if a familiar and rational and rule-based (and in this case Left-leaning) form of textual analysis suddenly seemed brittle when brought to bear on political reality, would critics finding this to be so, be forced to choose their tribe, in however small a measure? Was a subtle and incremental dynamic at work that would *position* intellectuals, helpless to resist, in the new bipolar world?

It is this dilemma that brings novelists and critics together, in a shared anxiety about the function of writing, and of cultural and critical commentary more generally. In this connection, Claire Messud's *The Emperor's Children* (2006) is an interesting book, with a tone set by 9/11, which transforms a satirical comedy of New York manners into a deliberation on the ethics and purpose of cultural work in the new world order. Messud's cast of characters are mostly on the same, broad professional quest, to be successful writers, of one kind or another. In a novel about surface and depth, the nature of 'success' is the focus of the satire; but it is also at the heart of the seriousness, less easily categorized, that finally emerges.

The events of 9/11 unfold towards the end of the novel, producing some points of clarification for the characters in pursuit of their personal goals, but also highlighting the triviality of their world. This serves the purpose of emphasizing the fragility of pre-9/11 society; but it runs the risk of making the social landscape of Messud's novel – and the light narrative style she utilizes to capture it – seem brittle as well.

At the heart of the novel is the famous and much-respected cultural commentator Murray Thwaite, formerly a front-line news reporter, whose twelfth and most recent book is an analysis of late capitalism. Murray is a portrait of a man resting on his laurels, falling into habits of duplicity and infidelity, recycling material from his earlier writing, and generally failing to live up to his own exacting standards of pursuing the truth. Murray is the 'emperor', ripe for exposure, whose 'children' (including his daughter Marina) comprise the generation of would-be writers and commentators who work under his dominant influence, and whose work, bereft of substance, is stalled. Marina's best friends are: Danielle Mirkoff, an aspiring documentary producer who cannot get a worthwhile programme commissioned; and Julius Clarke, author of influential book reviews who cannot accomplish the feat of writing a novel of his own. Marina's creative stasis is the most pronounced: she has spent the best part of a decade failing to complete the sociological study that supplies Messud's title, 'The Emperor's Children Have no Clothes'.

The chief target of the satire is the Australian Ludovic Seeley, who relocates to New York to launch a 'revolutionary' journal entitled *The Monitor*, which is conceived as the vehicle of the biting cultural exposé. Yet his 'alternative morality', characterized in Danielle's reflection as the aim 'to get everyone to see another way, his way, and then to make that the standard' (p. 160), is an expression of trend-setting and media power, facilitated by the postmodern relativization of 'truth'. Murray is the particular object of Seeley's spleen, in a novel with a recurring Oedipal motif. Seeley marries Murray's daughter, and helps her to finish the book that might bring her out from her father's shadow. When asked to comment on the manuscript, Murray, ruthlessly faithful to his pursuit of truth, does little to temper his judgement: 'The Emperor's Children Have no Clothes', he has decided, consists of 'frothy waffle' and 'introductory sociology garbage' about the children's clothing market, and the sexualization of childhood (p. 287). His advice to Marina is 'to resist the temptation' to publish (p. 290).

The most important challenge to Murray's intellectual paternalism, however, comes from his nephew Bootie, a college drop-out who moves from the provinces to the city in the hope of advancing his self-education at Murray's feet. Taking pity on him, Murray employs Bootie as his secretary; but the idealistic acolyte is soon disillusioned with his role-model, especially after finding his secret and unfinished manuscript, a series of philosophical musings on the topic of 'How to Live'. Finding the manuscript vapid, and after witnessing Murray's hypocrisy first-hand, Bootie resolves to expose him, a self-destructive act for which he is cast out by the Thwaites.

The events of 9/11 provide a kind of catharsis. *The Monitor* is scrapped prior to its launch date (13 September), dismissed by the publisher as a 'frivolous, satirical thing' that nobody wants now. Also, Murray is reinvigorated. He abandons his affair with Danielle, and, finding himself 'called upon to provide moral or ethical guidance', he charts 'a reasoned middle ground', mindful of the 'persistent agonies of the West Bank' and the 'ever growing population of disenfranchised Muslim youth around the globe' (pp. 412–13). When questioned about his own 'personal tragedy' in a TV interview – Bootie is presumed to have been killed when the Twin Towers collapsed – he refuses to turn hawkish, which is taken as a mark of 'immovable integrity'. It is important that Murray is aware of the irony and falsity of this, and that the consequence is not opportunistic self-promotion, but a new resolve about his philosophical tract, 'How to Live', which he plans to reshape in the light of 9/11 and Bootie's death, perhaps making his nephew the dedicatee (p. 414).

Bootie is not dead, however. Rather, he takes the opportunity afforded by the chaos of 9/11 to flee New York and assume a new identity, the better to foment his genius and unleash it on an unsuspecting world. He has been curiously impressed and inspired by the power of the terrorist attack:

> It was an awesome, a fearful thought: you could make something inside your head, as huge and devastating as this, and spill it out into reality, make it really happen. You could – for evil, but if for evil, then why not for good, too? – change the world. How petty Uncle Murray appeared, next to this. (p. 395)

This reflection confirms Bootie's sense of his own incipient genius, waiting to be unleashed upon the world, the idea with which the novel ends. Once drawn to novels, Bootie now becomes a 'sleeper' in classic terrorist fashion, cut off from his family, undetectable by the authorities, and waiting for his genius to declare itself, presumably in some mode of writing he has yet to discover. The 'good' that Bootie intends to project is evidently tainted, however, by his zealotry and asocial behaviour. Messud seems here to be responding to Don DeLillo's *Mao II*, a novel that – in her husband James Wood's words – 'proposed the foolish notion that the terrorist now does what the novelist used to do, that is, "alter the inner life of the culture"'.[9]

We might pause to consider just how foolish this notion is. One of the characters in *Mao II* is the photographer Brita, four years into an apparently endless quest to photograph the world's writers, country by country. She is, she says, 'furnishing' her 'own kind of witness' in producing this 'planetary record' (p. 25). In a book haunted by the idea that 'the image world is corrupt', Brita's project is potentially redemptive, especially when she is seeking to capture the 'grace' and 'wholeness' of those reclusive writers who have made themselves 'inaccessible' (p. 36). One such novelist is Bill Gray, whose encounter with Brita sets him on a journey to Beirut to play a part in the release of a kidnapped fellow writer (more precisely, a UN worker who is the author of some occasional poetry). What he is really doing is acting out the sense of defeat pinpointed by Woods, and which is first articulated by Gray, in the photo-session with Brita, as an angry response to a world in which the image, and the news, produces a form of capitulation to terror:

> There's a curious knot that binds novelists and terrorists. In the West we become famous effigies as our books lose the power to shape and influence.... Years ago I used to think it was possible for a novelist to alter the inner life of the culture. Now bomb-makers and gunmen have taken that territory. They make raids on human consciousness. (p. 41)

Bill's editor – who is trying to engineer a publicity coup, involving Bill, in support of the kidnapped poet – refines this idea: 'we understand how reality is invented. A person sits in a room and thinks a thought and it bleeds out into the world. Every thought is permitted. And there's no longer a moral or spatial distinction between thinking and acting' (p. 132).

Earlier in the novel, Scott, Bill's secretary and right-hand man, quotes Bill to articulate the sense that the news has usurped the function of the novel, which 'used to feed our search for meaning'. Now, 'we turn to the news, which provides an unremitting mood of catastrophe' and 'emotional experience not available elsewhere'. Hence 'we don't need the novel', or, indeed the catastrophes themselves, since 'the reports and predictions and warnings' are sufficient to feed this new hunger for meaning (p. 72).

Mao II is written against this cultural development. For Bill (and DeLillo), the novel is ultimately a form that stands in opposition to systemic utopianism or fundamentalism, whether this is manifested in Mao's China, the teachings of Reverend Moon, or the terrorist mind-set encountered by Brita in Beirut in the novel's closing section. As Bill explains to the sinister George, intermediary for the hostage-takers, 'the experience of my own consciousness tells me how autocracy fails, how total control wrecks the spirit, how my characters deny my efforts to own them completely, how I need internal dissent, self-argument, how the world squashes me the minute I think it's mine.' This paean to the democratic spirit embodied in the novel as a form – and also in its availability, as a mode of expression, to 'almost any amateur off the street' (p. 159) – might seem to be over-shadowed in the novel's conclusion. Bill dies before reaching Beirut, and Brita's journey to the terrorist cell that Bill fails to reach shows us that she has abandoned her project to photograph writers, who no longer figure among 'the interesting things', it seems (p. 229).

In spite of its impetus, the novel enacts the usurpation of the novel's terrain – the world of consciousness, ideas – by the era of terror, and especially news of terror. Even so, it is worth remarking on the obvious irony that it takes a well-constructed novel to articulate such a moment so deftly, embracing the tension of ideological conflict, and conveying a mood of cultural despair.

Still more pessimistic, viewed with hindsight, is the element of prescience in *Mao II*. The skyline from Brita's New York loft apartment is dominated by the World Trade Centre, the Twin Towers 'intensely massed and near. This is the word "loomed" in all its prolonged and impending force' (p. 87). This brooding idea is revisited later in the novel when Brita recalls a painting called *Skyscraper III*, 'a panelled canvas showing the World Trade Center at precisely the angle she saw it from her window and in the same dark spirit. These were her towers, two black latex slabs that consumed the available space' (p. 165). Andy Warhol's pencil drawing *Mao II* is reinvoked here, as well as the painting of Gorbachev, *Gorby I*, a picture that goes 'beyond parody . . . and appropriation' of Warhol, but in which Brita finds 'all the death glamour' of Warhol's work. All the images seem to correspond with Brita's assessment of *Gorby I* as a 'maximum statement about the dissolvability of the artist and the exaltation of the public figure' (p. 134).

The association of the Twin Towers in this assessment, in which the artist cedes authority to the image (and the era of terror), is obviously arresting, with hindsight. *Mao II* was published in 1991, two years before the first Islamist attempt to blow up the Twin Towers in February 1993. One of the characters in DeLillo's later *Falling Man* (2007) reminds us of this prediction: 'Weren't the towers built as fantasies of wealth and power that would one day become fantasies of destruction? You build a thing like that so you can see it come down. The provocation is obvious' (p. 116). This character, Martin, has links with the 'German terrorists of the early seventies' (p. 147), and it is from this perspective that he interprets the Islamist attack on America in economic terms. Yet, for another character, Lianne, this distinguishes him from the Islamists, making him – if he was once a terrorist – 'one of ours, which meant godless, Western, white' (p. 195). The Marxian interpretation haunts the novel, as when Lianne is called upon to speak to the participants in the workshop she runs for dementia sufferers, who look to her 'for words from her side of the line, where what is solid does not melt' (p. 127). This allusion to Marx's figure for the endless destruction and reconstruction on which capitalism is based – all that is solid melts into air – does some complex work, here. The uncertainty of the city 'after the planes' may betray a collective dawning awareness that the principle of capitalist growth, made manifest in perpetual demolition and rebuilding, may have been turned in on itself by the attack on the World Trade Centre. The dementia of the workshop participants may then represent a broader loss of faith in past certainties.

The falling man of the novel is, ostensibly, the performance artist so named, who appears unannounced across New York following the attack on the World Trade Centre, dangling from a wire wearing 'a business suit, one leg bent up, arms at his side'. His performances are a raw reminder of the office workers who fell to their deaths from the Twin Towers, and the haunting media images of these deaths that are already brought instantly to mind by the title of DeLillo's novel. Falling Man's signature pose is apparently modelled on one of the most infamous of these images (depicting a restaurant worker), a gesture that highlights the issue that torments DeLillo, and other novelists confronted by the unavoidable centrality of 9/11 to American consciousness: what does it mean to aestheticize these events by incorporating them in the form of a novel? (pp. 33, 222). The fate of Falling Man, pieced together by Lianne from Internet articles, may give an indication of DeLillo's meaning: rather than a provocative acrobat, he apparently sacrifices himself to the gesture of this performance, the repeated 'painful and highly dangerous' falls involving 'rudimentary equipment', which have resulted in a spinal injury and a related 'chronic depression'. He dies at 39, before making his planned final jump without a harness (pp. 218–24).[10]

This suicide-as-performance suggests a variation on the connection made in *Mao II* between the terrorist and the artist/novelist. Here, the suicide performer is an inverted reaction to the suicide bombers of 9/11, pushing art beyond aesthetics to a form of witness that is self-destructive. There is surely an intended parallel with the novel in which Falling Man appears, a novel haunted by the risk of aestheticizing a national trauma, but which responds to that risk not by looking away, but by looking so directly at it that the recognizable framework of a novel dissolves. The effect is a work that registers the seismic impact on the culture, especially in terms of psychology and domesticity. Keith Neudecker, the 9/11 survivor at the heart of this novel, is another falling man. In the aftermath of the disaster, he seeks out his estranged wife and son, and they reconnect; but there is a sense in which this rediscovery of domestic order is a parody of a former life, a desperate clutching at the past. Keith's new career, as an itinerant poker player, may also be taken as a vulgar expression of an economic system sustained by financial speculation and symbolized in the Twin Towers. DeLillo depicts a culture reasserting itself in reaction to the attack, but in the form of self-caricature, that is also knowingly self-destructive.

Something of that impression is conveyed by the novel, taken as a whole: DeLillo's descriptive skills, which have made him a master of the set piece, are inevitably turned on the immediate aftermath of 9/11, and the hellish scenes as the towers fall. DeLillo's topic obliges him to do this, and the result is somehow visceral, beyond the normal bounds of novel-writing. *Falling Man* attempts to recontain 9/11 through its descriptive brilliance and its emotional charge; yet it also demonstrates the impossibility of any such recontainment. This paradox may constitute the most effective and appropriate response of the major American novelist, writing from the point of view of a culture momentarily shaken to its foundations: another perspective seems unavailable, as the unconvincing episodes in *Falling Man* involving the 9/11 terrorists suggest.

Messud and DeLillo both register a perceived devaluing of artistic work, and of cultural commentary more generally, in response to terrorism, which becomes a new and overshadowing cultural dominant. For the literary critic, there is an equivalent sense of displacement, since the symptomatic reading that we might expect to see much of in the treatment of post-9/11 writing may incline the critic towards the complicity of a Marcia Umanoff. This danger, together with the alternative impulse, of passive reception, establishes the Scylla and Charybdis the critic must now negotiate to establish a meaningful intervention.

The emphasis on the falling man in the American novel helps us to chart a course. In *Extremely Loud and Incredibly Close* (2005) Jonathan Safran Foer had already made this iconic image a point of focus. Like DeLillo's, his treatment tests the capacity of the novel to make an aesthetic response to a broad-based social trauma. The central character

139

is the Manhattan nine-year-old Oskar Schell, who is intelligent yet nerdish, so that he is winning with adults, but ridiculed by his peers. Leaving aside some of the improbabilities of this character, the interesting aspect of Safran Foer's composition is the attempt to generate empathy for the loss suffered by a child who is at once too intelligent yet insufficiently mature to cope with that loss. The question of the book's success or failure with readers then depends upon the degree to which they are prepared to accept this premise: some will find it affecting, some cloying. However, it may be the larger allegorical dimension to this that is interesting: like this insulated nine-year-old, many ordinary Americans had to wake up to a political reality that was hard to grasp, after 9/11.

Oskar's father is killed in the attacks, trapped in the restaurant at the top of the north tower of the World Trade Centre when the first plane strikes. Oskar is haunted by a series of phone messages left by his father – the person he loved most – calling to give reassurance, even when the situation evidently becomes hopeless. Oskar is sent home from school, and arrives as his father continues to call, but is frozen, unable to answer. It subsequently transpires that his father also called Oskar's mother on her cellphone: the messages at home were specifically for his son. The novel broadens its poignant treatment of the lost connection between father and son to embrace Oskar's lost grandfather Thomas, emotionally traumatized himself in the aftermath of the bombing of Dresden, and who comes back to his family only after the son he never knew is dead. The widening of the historical lens to embrace the Second World War – including the Nazi Holocaust and Hiroshima – reveals a treatment designed to underscore the personal suffering engendered by political extremism.

Yet it is the immediate context of 9/11 that gives this novel its significance, and especially through its risky engagement with those publicly shared signs of trauma. The cellphone calls were one of these; the falling bodies another. Both are fictionalized by Safran Foer, for Oskar is also haunted by one particular image of a falling body – which, he speculates, could have been his father – and which he prints for his scrapbook ('Stuff That Happened to Me'), in a series of stills showing the fall downloaded from the Internet. The various other images from the scrapbook, an externalized record of a mind in confusion and emotional turmoil, are reproduced throughout the novel, a gesture that seeks to infuse with affect a familiar form of postmodern jokiness. But it is the series of pictures showing the falling body to which Oskar returns at the end of the novel, when his scrapbook is full:

> Was it Dad?
> Maybe.
> Whoever it was, it was somebody.
> I ripped the pages out of the book.
> I reversed the order, so the last one was first, and the first last.
> When I flipped through them, it looked like the man was floating up through the sky. (p. 325)

The novel closes in the manner of Amis's *Time's Arrow* with Oskar's conceit extended so that his father moves further and further away from the point of the attack, and is safe. This is an enormously affecting close to the novel; but the final pages then reproduce the 'flick book' that Oskar has described: the reader's final act is to create the illusion of the body flying upwards, a textual trick that lowers the emotional intensity of the closing page, and hands back judgement to the reader. We are expressly invited to consider if this kind of visual play is appropriate for this event. Anticipating DeLillo's *Falling Man*, Safran Foer finds a way of demonstrating the limits of the novel's ability to give an acceptable aesthetic shape to the events of 9/11. Yet he also creates a cultural record that may well be judged differently as those events recede from the collective memory. It will be interesting to see how this novel is read in ten or twenty years, as an investigation of the novel's capacity to engage a large political canvas.

The recurrence of the image of the falling man in the post-9/11 American novel is comparable with the obsession with the plane in post-9/11 British novels (such as McEwan's *Saturday* and Amis's *Yellow Dog*). At a time when popular anti-Iraq war sentiment, especially in America, was seizing on quite different images – notably the hooded Abu Ghraib prisoner – as symbols of American imperialism, novelists were still exploring the trauma generated by the attack on America. From one academic perspective, the novelists' view might seem to epitomize the 'nauseating media reception' condemned at the outset by Jameson. A politicized perspective on 9/11 and its aftermath might then be revealed by which symbolic figure, Falling Man or Abu Ghraib Man, is first brought to mind.

More temperately, the preoccupations of DeLillo and Safran Foer suggest a stage of 'taking stock' in the American novel, a moment where national identity is shaken, and the novelist, quite properly, responds. There is also a potential double bind here: the novelist either betrays public sentiment, or is deemed to pander to it so that a 'Western' cultural perspective on terror is positioned in advance. The problem for defenders of the novel is that, since the international outcry over *The Satanic Verses*, this is an art form that has come to epitomize a caricatured notion of Western godlessness in the Islamic world (and not just in the minds of Islamists). There is a matter of principle at stake, here, with a global dimension; but it may be better to avoid the confrontational manner of putting the case.

The pitfalls of confrontation are clear from Martin Amis's recent loss of critical distance. His attacks on Islamism appear to have grown out of his vitriolic condemnations of Stalin in *Koba the Dread* (2002), and the novel *House of Meetings* (2006). Commenting on this phase of his work, and on Amis's increasingly strident pronouncements about Islam, Daniel Soar detects a loss of 'lightness' in the treatment of hatred: 'one benefit of the Amisian lightly ironizing put-down was to deny a hatred the fuel it gains from being taken seriously.'[11] Amis now clearly feels blunt rhetorical tools to be necessary. The polemical fuel that drives his essay 'The Age of Horrorism', for example, is based on affiliation and the necessity of confrontation – 'our ideology, which is sometimes called Westernism', he writes – and the need to overcome the disabling relativism of that 'Western' perspective, which 'weakens our morality and will'. The appeal to Conrad's celebration of the marvellous living world at the end of the essay (in the 'Author's Note' to *The Shadow-Line*) deliberately situates the English novel as a combatant in the new global war of ideologies, and more particularly, as an aesthetic form that enshrines a secular worldview, making it worthy of reverence on that basis.[12]

To take up the challenge in this way is fraught with difficulty, because it accepts the false opposition – between Islam and 'the West' – that Islamists seek to impose on the world. As I indicated in the previous chapter, what is required is a quiet rejection of the standoff, and a slow dismantling of the construction of 'the West'. With such a project in mind, it may be that academic criticism of the novel can now come in to its own by reasserting the independent position of judgement that *should* be the privilege of university life in any national context, though this will be hard to achieve. For novelists, a credible position of independence will be equally hard-won.

A novel that dramatizes this problem of perspective – the new cultural tribalism – is Mohsin Hamid's *The Reluctant Fundamentalist* (2007), a tense novel narrated by a young Pakistani called Changez, from a once-important family. He is a Princeton graduate, and a highly paid financial consultant based in New York: a cosmopolitan figure from the upper echelons of Third World society, able to advance rapidly in the economic global village because of the cultural capital that attaches to his outsider status. The real relations of this exoticization are exposed by the events of 9/11. Changez relates his reaction to the attack, viewing the footage in his hotel bedroom while on business in Manila, and the mask of the subaltern slips: 'I stared as one – and then the other – of the twin towers of New York's World Trade Center collapsed. And then I smiled. Yes, despicable as it may sound, my initial reaction was to be remarkably pleased' (p. 72). On the same trip, he has already been shaken by the hostile glare of a jeepney driver, with whom he finds he 'shared a sort of Third World sensibility'. He finds himself appraising a colleague with the same eye the local driver had turned on him, an eye that registers foreignness (p. 67).

It is the nature of his work – for a valuation firm assessing large business concerns – that provokes Changez's identity crisis. The economic imperialism that he facilitates is crystallized for him while on his final job for the firm, assessing a Chilean publisher. The publishing company's chief, fearful that the sale of the company will signal the end of its (loss-making) literary publishing, currently subsidized by other ventures, recognizes the chink in Changez's armour. He exploits this by reminding Changez of the janissaries, those Christians captured by the Ottomans and turned into a ferocious Muslim army: they 'fought to erase their own civilizations', an activity Changez realizes he is also engaged in (p. 151); and this establishes an important principle of reversal that lends this novel its importance.

The events of 9/11 make America in general, and New York in particular, far less welcoming for Changez. He had formerly been comfortable wearing a 'starched white kurta' on the subway in New York, a city he had experienced as open-minded and 'cosmopolitan' (p. 48). After the attack on America, however, he is treated with hostility and suspicion, and retreats into his ethnic identity, the external manifestation of which is the beard that exposes him to further prejudice. It is that principle of reversal, however, that lifts the novel from the morass of tribalism. Indeed, the significant aspect of *The Reluctant Fundamentalist* is the manner in which it progresses beyond the simple tale that readers will start to detect, the tale of resentment and alienation bred by discrimination and intolerance. The title, of course, raises just this spectre, of a narrative of a Pakistani man's retreat into Islamism, having been courted then rejected by the West. But Changez's new direction stems from a self-revelation that begins prior to 9/11, and which sees him turn from the parasitical world of high finance, and the 'fundamentals' of economic science. The imperative to 'focus on the fundamentals', as the 'grounding principle' in valuation work, 'mandated a single-minded attention to financial detail' (p. 98); and this floats the idea of opposing principles of fundamentalism.

If this is a little obvious, it works because the book is designed to challenge the static binarism that responses to 9/11 have often invited or imposed. Indeed, the literary device of reversal is used to telling effect, especially for an American audience. The frame for the novel is the conceit that Changez is narrating his life story to an American, in a restaurant in Lahore, over the course of a single evening, a few years after 9/11. Changez has returned to Pakistan as a university lecturer, and has a growing reputation as a radical. At the end of the evening he accompanies the American to his hotel, and they are followed by a number of men, including the waiter who has served them earlier. The novel ends as these figures close in on Changez and the American, leaving the suspense unresolved. The reader anticipates a mugging, or a kidnapping, or a killing; but it is unclear who will dispense the violence, whether the American is an undercover assassin, or Changez is a terrorist.

The action, then, enacts the defeat of cosmopolitan New York, and the rise of a cultural binarism conceived as opposing 'fundamental' systems – with the system Changez has extricated himself from pointedly involved in the disregard of international literary publishing, blind to its value beyond the fundamental rules of commerce. The principle of reversal then unsettles this binarism, making Hamid's novel a purposive cosmopolitan effort, and a demonstration of the value of the literary response in this context.

Once again, the idea of cosmopolitanism, generated self-consciously, seems to be the best resource for side-stepping the ideological impasse that Amis has willingly accepted, and which momentarily seemed to stall the novel in Britain and America at the beginning of the century. In different versions, a notion of cosmopolitan identity might also suggest a necessary reorientation of the other identities at stake in this book: that of the academic literary critic; and, most crucially, the construction of the new global citizen.

One group that might seem peculiarly intransigent to this notion of cosmopolitanism, conceived as a way of advancing the aims of an inclusive multiculturalism, is the Muslim community in Britain. The monumental problems that have to be addressed for this utopian inclusiveness to embrace this community are laid bare in Ed Husain's important personal testimony about radical Islam in Britain. Husain shows that the appeal of Islamist ideology reveals a generational divide; but it is the way it has insinuated itself into more moderate Muslim thought that signals his chief concern. He is also clearly dismayed by the way in which leading Muslim figures and organizations, including those consulted by government, are characterized by an Islamist drive beneath their sanitized public pronouncements, a form of 'doublespeak' he presents as endemic (p. 282).

145

Husain shows how the key tenets of Islamism are flourishing in British Muslim communities, especially in the minds of the impressionable young, vulnerable to aggressive recruitment techniques, often sponsored from abroad: these tenets, including a virulent anti-Semitism, and a conviction of Muslim superiority, stem from a belief in the *ummah*, the global Muslim nation, which renders any other kind of national feeling improper. Allied to this, the presentation of political democracy as 'idolatrous' frees the would-be radical to dismiss British law as an impediment to his religious duties to help establish the global Muslim nation by force. The implicit goal of global domination is epitomized, with disturbingly deliberate historical echoes, in a radical student poster from the 1990s: 'Islam: The Final Solution' (p. 54).

Husain points out that there are grounds for hope – that, indeed, a good measure of beneficent multiculturalism is evidenced in the lives of British Muslims 'incorporating the best aspects of their multifaceted heritage: ethnic ancestry, British upbringing, Islamic roots.' It is this 'silent majority of law-abiding and loyal Muslims', working in 'core areas of national life', who are the 'true heroes of British Islam'.[13] This hope, however, seems to hinge on a resurgence of spiritual Islam, and the defeat of those ideologues who have appropriated Islam for political purposes on a world stage. In that latter view, the very idea of British multiculturalism is anathema. This makes the growth of multiculturalism in particular Muslim communities improbable. Husain's own experiences in the East End of London – recruiting for the Islamist cause in Tower Hamlets, shifting his allegiance from the Brick Lane mosque to the nearby East London mosque at one stage of his radicalization – makes the very idea that the area including Brick Lane should be a focus for debates about multiculturalism seem fanciful. Yet the historical experience of Brick Lane, considered in chapter three, reveals it to be both a doorway of gradual integration for successive migrant groups, and also a source of slow cultural enrichment for the wider society.

Such a process of enrichment is one aspect of the worthwhile form of cosmopolitanism, rooted in cultural and ethnic diversity, that must be embraced. Yet cosmopolitanism has been variously condemned by postcolonial literary critics. Certainly, it should be acknowledged that

146

the concept has both positive and negative associations. In various contexts, 'the cosmopolitan' has been 'the target of xenophobia, disrespect, suspicion, and mistrust', while cosmopolitanism also evokes the 'culturally sophisticated' citizen who stands in contrast to 'the provincial and naïve'; yet, the celebratory view also brings with it the suspicion of an 'elite aesthetic'.[14] The tension between the local and the global implied in those opposed perspectives on cosmopolitanism reveals the potential of the concept in the historical moment of globalization: to highlight the interaction between national and transnational impulses which necessarily come under scrutiny in any analysis of global politics. It is this very tension, moreover, that pinpoints the current crossroads of the novel.

In the fields of philosophy, political science and sociology, cosmopolitanism is beginning to emerge as a transcendent idea that might enshrine some necessary principles of global social justice and order. For moral philosophers, cosmopolitanism can define current responsibilities by highlighting 'the obligations we have to those whom we do not know, and with whom we are not intimate, but whose lives touch ours sufficiently that what we do can affect them.'[15] In its 'strong' form, this cosmopolitanism requires that global questions of responsibility will always take precedence over national obligations, where the issues of wealth, resources and equality are concerned, because 'there are no society-wide principles of distributive justice that are not also global principles of distributive justice'.[16]

In a more nuanced view, cosmopolitans should seek to 'accommodate and account for national allegiances without compromising their motivating and fundamental commitment to global equality.' Such a challenge must be met because 'a theory of global justice that does not accommodate and properly account for the special ties and obligations of shared nationality would not be a theory of justice suited for humanity.' The way to reconcile the two, however, may involve 'subordinating the claims of nationality to the claims of cosmopolitan justice.'[17]

The tension between the local and the global, the national and the transnational, becomes especially pressing in the context of the post-9/11 world. For Ulrich Beck, 'the human condition has ... become cosmopolitan' in a context where 'the most recent avatar in

147

the genealogy of global risks, the threat of terror, also knows no borders.' By the same token, the international protest against the Iraq war underscores the paradox, already evident, 'that resistance against globalization itself produces political globalization'.

If there is an 'internal cosmopolitanization' of national institutions, or institutions within nation-states, that process might not always be benign, as in Ed Husain's account of the radicalization of young Muslim men in Britain, taking up arms in the name of the global Islamic nation. Husain's appeal to a *de facto* form of multiculturalism within the nation-state, established over generations, is the primary route through which the moral responsibility of would-be militants might be established.

In fact, Beck's conception of the cosmopolitan vision, though fundamentally opposed to narrow and delimited forms of nationalism, is able to embrace the indeterminacy and the potential contradiction of the life actually lived, most clearly in what he calls 'the mélange principle', that 'local, national, ethnic, religious and cosmopolitan cultures and traditions interpenetrate, interconnect and intermingle'.[18]

The postcolonial moment of the latter stages of the twentieth century is, for Beck, 'another factor in the rise of cosmopolitanism', and a more positive idea if viewed through the proper historical lens: postcolonial discourse should oblige us to understand how 'the "European self" is ... interwoven with the "excluded others" of the colonized world', with a transformative effect on 'European self-understanding'. The effect should be that of 'opening and expanding the national into a cosmopolitan Europe.'[19]

It is cosmopolitanism in this spirit that inspires Rose Tremain's powerful novel about economic migrancy, *The Road Home* (2007). This is a fitting book with which to end this survey, because it is precisely the kind of novel that academic readers have trouble with, despite the approval of a broader readership.[20] Most of the narrative is filtered through the consciousness of the central character, Lev, a widower in his forties, forced to leave his village in Eastern Europe (probably Poland) to support his mother and daughter. His wife was a cancer victim, in a polluted region rife with the disease, and the local sawmill where he worked has closed down, due to rapid deforestation. The early episodes of the book, as Lev tries to make his way in London, create a vivid sense of misery and hardship for the economic migrant in a hostile city. Yet his own determination (and personal appeal), coupled with the kindness and assistance of others, set him on a path of recuperation through intensive hard work.

There are two psychological hurdles he must overcome: first, he must begin to vanquish his grief over his lost wife, which he begins to do when he finds himself ready to embark on a relationship with a co-worker in the kitchen of a fashionable London restaurant. The second obstacle is a loss of faith in the idea of 'home'. This begins to acquire fresh significance for him when his village, Auror, is threatened by the proposed construction of a dam. He hatches the plan of using the expertise he has acquired in his time in London – working in three kitchens, eventually as a chef – to open a restaurant in the town of Baryn (to become 'New Baryn') to which the villagers will be forced to relocate. In the conclusion of the novel, this plan is realized. Lev is reunited with his daughter, and the best friend who was beginning to feel betrayed, and their restaurant becomes a success, on the tide of prosperity the dam and hydro-electric project has brought to the region: 'Auror', Lev comes to realize, 'was a place so lonely, so abandoned by time, it was right to drown it, right to force its inhabitants to leave behind their dirt roads . . . and join the twenty-first-century world' (p. 344).

The trajectory of Lev's return journey from Auror to London, ostensibly a process of embracing globalization, is not a straightforward matter, however. Having progressed to the station of vegetable preparation in the fashionable London restaurant, and in the midst of a passionate relationship with Sophie, the sous-chef, he reaches the true nadir of his journey. She throws Lev over for a celebrity conceptual artist, Howie Preece, and it is his set – which includes a 'cutting edge' playwright – that bears the brunt of the book's satire, and which eventually contributes to a nuanced presentation of globalization and cosmopolitanism. The world of the smart London set is rooted in their self-consciousness about *being* 'cutting edge'; this is a form of celebrity art that displaces personal values (p. 210). It also displaces the material fact of work, in stark contrast to the experiences of the economic migrant, since the 'concepts' of the artist are realized by studio assistants rather than by the artist himself.

This becomes important when an art gallery opens next door to Lev's restaurant in New Baryn. In the window is placed a sculpture, 'resembling a human torso sliced in half', made from car parts. This incenses Lev's friend (and now maître d') Rudi: his way of dealing with economic hardship has been to buy an old Chevrolet and run a taxi business, despite the huge difficulty and anxiety of keeping the vehicle on the road in the absence of available spare parts. The restaurant itself is in the premises of a former garage, closed due to economic decline. In this context, Rudi thinks the 'squandering' of auto parts in a sculpture, 'as though they had no value', is 'degenerate' (p. 360).

There is a distinction, of course, between the London art world, satirized as a branch of celebrity culture, and the exportation of this mechanical sculpture to Eastern Europe, where industry directly determines and delimits lives, whether through the availability of work, enforced relocation, or pollution. From this perspective, the sculpture might be seen to raise some tough questions about artistic value, which have a genuine bearing on New Baryn. There is also an invitation for us to think about the 'product' Lev has imported into his restaurant next door. He has learnt much from the celebrated London chef G. K. Ashe, heavily influenced by French cuisine; but it is the principle of using fresh, locally sourced produce that he 'imports'. This would seem to be a new (and paradoxically) cosmopolitan principle that has local benefits, though Lev really has no choice other than to rely on local suppliers. He has also, however, learnt much from a Greek restaurateur about striking a balance between the preservation and adaptation of traditional culture. It is this aspect of his migrant experience that seems especially relevant to the stabilization of his venture in 'a world slipping and sliding on a precipice between the dark rockface of Communism and the seductive, light-filled void of the liberal market' (p. 337).

In the bleakest phase of the novel, Lev is sacked by G. K. Ashe (who does not wish the emotional fall-out from Lev's relationship with his sous-chef to impact on his kitchen), and goes to work as a vegetable picker in Suffolk. This intensive and poorly paid labour, now the preserve of the migrant worker, gives a thoughtful inflexion to the novel's treatment of cosmopolitanism articulated through the treatment of restaurant culture. As with the representation of art, there is a sense that the genuine cosmopolitanism is happening away from the 'cosmopolitan' centre. Where the British experience resonates with exploitation, the development Lev pioneers in New Baryn, working directly with local suppliers to build a better chain, seems productive for the community, with no visible signs of exploitation. In this conception of cosmopolitanism, it is the dismantling of the distinction between centre and periphery, in terms of purpose and economic prosperity, that resonates.

Against the idea of cosmopolitan elitism, Kwame Anthony Appiah points out that economic migrancy is a prime motivator in the production of cultural hybridity: 'most of those who have learned the languages and customs of other places haven't done so out of mere curiosity. A few were looking for food for thought; most were looking for food.' By the same token, a *lack* of cosmopolitanism can be the sign of a more worrying form of elitism: 'thoroughgoing ignorance about the ways of others is largely a privilege of the powerful.'[21]

Tremain's cosmopolitanism, rooted in principles of communal responsibility and hard graft, is also fragile, vulnerable to the vicissitudes of economic circumstance. But that, of course, is the context we are being asked to understand. For a British audience, the novel amounts to a contemporary fable of migrancy that will remind readers of their own global obligations. The 'road home' is then a return to principles of moral responsibility in a new global context. This cosmopolitanism should be the orientation that unites novelists, readers and critics in the twenty-first century, a stance characterized by an openness to pluralism, and an accompanying humility, or a willingness to develop in unforeseen directions. A cosmopolitan criticism will read partially 'with-the-grain', recognizing those vital contextual forces that create tensions between national and international impulses. And there will need to be a clear understanding that a worthwhile form of cosmopolitanism is already shot-through with provincialism, just as an enriching form of provincialism is always inflected with a cosmopolitan worldview.

151

Notes

Introduction

1   In this discussion, I am drawing on John Frow's book, *Cultural Studies and Cultural Value* (Oxford: Oxford University Press, 1995).

2   Frow, *Cultural Studies and Cultural Value*, p. 165.

3   Bruce Robbins, *Secular Vocations: Intellectuals, Professionalism, Culture* (London: Verso, 1993), p. 223.

4   Robbins, *Secular Vocations*, p. 59. Robbins is following Raymond Williams's lament about critical distance, especially in his essay 'Beyond Cambridge English', reprinted in the collection *Writing in Society* (London: Verso, 1983).

5   John Brannigan, *Orwell to the Present: Literature in England, 1945–2000* (Basingstoke: Palgrave Macmillan, 2003), pp. 12, 204.

6   Peter Childs, *Contemporary Novelists: British Fiction Since 1970* (Basingstoke: Palgrave Macmillan, 2005), p. 1.

7   John Brockman, *The Third Culture: Beyond the Scientific Revolution* (New York: Simon and Schuster, 1995), p. 18.

8   Jago Morrison, *Contemporary Fiction* (London: Routledge, 2003), pp. 5–6.

9   Rod Liddle, 'Comment', *The Sunday Times*, 'Culture', 14 January 2007, pp. 6–7.

10   Nick Hornby, *The Complete Polysyllabic Spree* (London: Viking, 2006), pp. 24, 8.

11   Iris Murdoch, 'Against Dryness: A Polemical Sketch', in Malcolm Bradbury (ed.), *The Novel Today: Contemporary Writers on Modern Fiction*, revd edn (London: Fontana, 1990), pp. 15–24.

12   Robert Macfarlane, 'The World at Arm's Length', *Times Literary Supplement*, 5331, 3 June 2005, p. 19.

13   David Grylls, 'Not Waving but Drowning', *The Sunday Times*, 'Culture', 12 June 2005, p. 53.

14   See, for example, Sean O'Brien, 'Toppers' Talk', *Times Literary Supplement*, 5327, 6 May 2005, p. 20.

15   O'Brien, 'Toppers' Talk'.

16 Ian Sansom, 'Emotional Sushi', *London Review of Books*, 23: 15, 9 August 2001, pp. 19–20.

17 Robert McCrum, 'The Human Factor', *Observer*, 'Review', 27 May 2001, p. 15.

18 Trevor Lewis, 'At a glance' [untitled short review], *The Sunday Times*, 'Culture', 25 June 2006, p. 55.

19 Frank Cottrell Boyce, 'How to be Good', *Guardian*, 'Review', 10 June 2006, p. 16.

20 Cottrell Boyce, 'How to be Good'.

21 Jessica Olin, 'Feral Chihuahuas', *London Review of Books*, 28: 12, 22 June 2006, pp. 13–14.

Chapter 1 The Post-Consensus Renaissance?

1 James F. English, 'Introduction: British Fiction in a Global Context', in *A Concise Companion to Contemporary British Fiction*, ed. English (Oxford: Blackwell, 2006), pp. 1–15.

2 Ian McEwan and Kazuo Ishiguro were both students on the renowned MA programme in creative writing at UEA, pioneered by Malcolm Bradbury and Angus Wilson.

3 Nick Bentley (ed.), *British Fiction of the 1990s* (London: Routledge, 2005). In the introduction, Bentley indicates that the volume is predicated on the 'recognizable differences in British society and culture between the 1980s and 1990s that are reflected in the fiction of the period' (p. 2).

4 McEwan is quoting Halliday verbatim. See Fred Halliday, *Two Hours That Shook the World, September 11, 2001: Causes and Consequences* (London: Saqi Books, 2002), p. 24.

5 See Raymond Williams, *Politics and Letters: Interviews with 'New Left Review'* (London: New Left Books, 1979), p. 271.

6 Peter Childs, *Contemporary Novelists: British Fiction Since 1970* (Basingstoke: Palgrave Macmillan, 2005), p. 3.

7 Richard Todd, *Consuming Fictions: The Booker Prize and Fiction in Britain Today* (London: Bloomsbury, 1996), p. 8.

8 John Brannigan, *Orwell to the Present: Literature in England, 1945–2000* (Basingstoke: Palgrave Macmillan, 2003), p. 9.

9 Rubin Rabinovitz, *The Reaction Against Experiment in the English Novel, 1950–1960* (New York: Columbia University Press, 1967), pp. 168, 170.

10 Rabinovitz, *The Reaction Against Experiment*, p. 16.

11 See Andrzej Gasiorek, *Post-War British Fiction: Realism and After* (London: Edward Arnold, 1995).

12 For example, such an intrusive narrator interrupts the narrative occasionally throughout Drabble's trilogy of novels *The Radiant Way* (1987), *A Natural Curiosity* (1989) and *The Gates of Ivory* (1991).

13 I am thinking of the character Miss Porntip, stereotypical if not absurd, who emerges as an emblem of seductive, unfettered capitalism.

14 Brian W. Shaffer, *Reading the Novel in English, 1950–2000* (Oxford: Blackwell, 2006), pp. 1, 5, 10, 22.

15 The posthumous publication of the second volume of journals revealed him to be anti-semitic, homophobic, and vitriolic towards his wife, for many commentators. Ian Sansom's review of the first volume sums up the perception of unrelenting bile: 'if he doesn't hate you, Fowles probably wants to have sex with you; though as anyone who has read *The Collector* will know, these two things are intimately connected in the author's mind.' See 'His Own Peak', *London Review of Books*, 26: 9, 6 May 2004, pp. 32–3.

16 Hal Jensen, 'All Endeavour Useless', *Times Literary Supplement*, 5374, 31 March 2004, p. 20.

17 As Peter Mudford points out, Greene was engaging with the particular inflexion of this angst faced by Catholic Europe in the 1930s. See his *Graham Greene* (Plymouth: Northcote House, 1996), p. 22.

18 Daniel Lea draws an instructive parallel between Eliot's poem and Swift's novel in *Graham Swift* (Manchester: Manchester University Press, 2005), pp. 161–2.

19 John K. Walton, *The British Seaside: Holidays and Resorts in the Twentieth Century* (Manchester: Manchester University Press, 2000), pp. 196, 198.

20 Walton, *The British Seaside*, p. 3.

21 Walton, *The British Seaside*, pp. 3–4.

22 Walton, *The British Seaside*, p. 3.

23 Walton, *The British Seaside*, p. 69.

24 Paul Binding, 'Upwardly-Mobile Men out of Wells', *Times Literary Supplement*, 4969, 26 September 1998, p. 27.

Chapter 2   The Novel and Cultural Life in Britain

1 John Carey, *What Good are the Arts?* (London: Faber and Faber, 2005), pp. 27, 29–30.

2 David Hopkins, *After Modern Art: 1945–2000* (Oxford: Oxford University Press, 2000), p. 214.

3 The impact of the club has, arguably, made Richard and Judy 'the most power-ful people in publishing.' See www.books.guardian.co.uk/departments/generalfiction/story/0,6000,1156756,00.html (12.1.07).

4 Malcolm Bradbury, *The Modern British Novel* (London: Secker and Warburg, 1993), pp. 380, 381. In the later revised edition of this work the wording is different, but the judgement essentially the same. See *The Modern British Novel*, revised edition (London: Penguin, 2001), pp. 419–21.

5 Richard Todd, *Consuming Fictions: The Booker Prize and Fiction in Britain Today* (London: Bloomsbury, 1996), p. 8.

6   Todd, *Consuming Fictions*, p. 81. Todd cites the example of Penelope Lively's *Moon Tiger*, the 1987 winner, with its '"epic" qualities' and 'exotic setting'.

7   Clive Bloom, *Literature, Politics and Intellectual Crisis in Britain Today* (Basingstoke: Palgrave, 2001), pp. 91, 92.

8   Bloom, *Literature, Politics and Intellectual Crisis*, pp. 94, 108, 110.

9   James F. English, *The Economy of Prestige: Prizes, Awards, and the Circulation of Cultural Value* (Cambridge, MA: Harvard University Press, 2005), pp. 4, 7, 10.

10 See Bloom, *Literature, Politics and Intellectual Crisis*, p. 96.

11 Todd, *Consuming Fictions*, p. 74.

12 There were three other established authors on the 1998 shortlist who had not won the Booker, and who had also been shortlisted before: Beryl Bainbridge, Julian Barnes and Patrick McCabe. 1998 was the fifth time Bainbridge had been in contention for the prize, and she was considered the favourite by many commentators. McEwan's success was not well received: Will Self, on the live TV broadcast, found occasion 'to do his nut', in the words of Nicholas Lezard. See Lezard, 'Morality Bites', *Guardian*, 'Saturday Review', 24 April 1999, p. 11. *On Chesil Beach*, another McEwan novella, was shortlisted in 2007.

13 Juliet Waters, 'The Little Chill: Has the Booker Prize Chosen the Noveau Beaujolais of Fiction?', www.montrealmirror.com/ARCHIVES/1998/120398/book.html (13.7.05).

14 Graham Huggan, *The Postcolonial Exotic: Marketing the Margins* (London: Routledge, 2001), pp. 105, 107.

15 English characterizes Booker Brothers as 'a food-products concern with sugar-cane operations in the Caribbean'; yet he also points out that Booker was already a diversified company, having links with the Jonathan Cape publishing house, the prime mover in establishing the Booker Prize. See English, *The Economy of Prestige*, p. 199.

16 Huggan, *The Postcolonial Exotic*, pp. 106, 110, 111, 115, 120.

17 The following winners spring to mind: John Berger's G (1972); Nadine Gordimer's *The Conservationist* (1974); Salman Rushdie's *Midnight's Children* (1981); and J. M. Coetzee's *Life and Times of Michael K* (1983). The shortlists betray a good sprinkling of further experimentation and innovation by (among others) Fay Weldon, Graham Swift, Julian Barnes and Martin Amis.

18 Reported in Lavinia Greacen's *J. G. Farrell: The Making of a Writer* (London: Bloomsbury, 1999), p. 277.

19 See Todd, *Consuming Fictions*, p. 76.

20 After the award of the prize, Kiran Desai remarked that 'the debt I owe to my mother is so profound that I feel the book is hers as much as mine'. See www.books.guardian.co.uk/print/0,,329597763–121825,00.html (11.12.06).

21 'A New King for the Congo: Mobutu and the Nihilism in Africa', in *'The Return of Eva Perón' and 'The Killings in Trinidad'* (Harmondsworth: Penguin, 1981), pp. 165–96.

22 'A New King for the Congo', p. 188.

23 'Conrad's Darkness', in *'The Return of Eva Perón' and 'The Killings in Trinidad'*, pp. 197–218.

24 Fawzia Mustafa, *V. S. Naipaul* (Cambridge: Cambridge University Press, 1995), pp. 118–19.

25 Bruce King, *The Internationalization of English Literature*, Oxford English Literary History, vol. 13: 1948–2000 (Oxford: Oxford University Press, 2004), p. 251. In another recent history, Martin's novel is one of a select few mentioned to illustrate how 'new realist fiction' describing black experiences 'continues to make an impact'. See C. L. Innes, *A History of Black and Asian Writing in Britain, 1700–2000* (Cambridge: Cambridge University Press, 2002), p. 243.

26 Olaudah Equiano (c. 1745–1797) and his friend Ottobah Cugoano (dates uncertain), neighbours in London for a time, were both ex-slaves who published important anti-slavery texts, and who were thus pioneering African men of letters in British culture.

27 Bruce King cites *Incomparable World* as an influence on David Dabydeen's *A Harlot's Progress*, for example. See *The Internationalization of English Literature*, p. 251.

28 See, for example, Selvon's creolization of novelistic diction in *The Lonely Londoners* (1956), or Smith's groundbreaking attempt to capture youth diction in *Bad Friday* (1982).

Chapter 3   Assimilating Multiculturalism

1 James F. English, *The Economy of Prestige: Prizes, Awards, and the Circulation of Cultural Value* (Cambridge, MA: Harvard University Press, 2005), p. 307. English is here summarizing one critique in an important account of 'Prizes and the Politics of World Culture'. See pp. 297–320.

2 Ian Jack, 'It's Only a Novel', *Guardian*, 'Review', 20 December 2003, p. 7.

3 Richard Lea, 'Local Protests Over Brick Lane Film', *Guardian*, Monday 17 July 2006, www.books.guardian.co.uk/print/0,,329531826–99819,00.html.

4 Richard Lea, 'Novelists Hit Back at Brick Lane Protestors', *Guardian*, 31 July 2006, www.books.guardian.co.uk/print/0,,329542510–99819,00.html.

5 Hasan Suroor, '"Battle of Brick Lane" Fizzles Out', *The Hindu*, 2 August 2006, www.hinduonnet.com/thehindu/thscrip/print.pl?file=2006080205071100. htm&date=2006/08/02/&prd=th&.

6 Lisa Appignanesi, 'PEN is Concerned About Protests Over the Filming of Monica Ali's Brick Lane', www.englishpen.org/news/monicaalisbricklane/.

7 Lea, 'Novelists Hit Back at Brick Lane Protestors'.

8 Lea, 'Local Protests Over Brick Lane Film'.

9 Suroor, '"Battle of Brick Lane" Fizzles Out'.

10 'Damp squib' was Salman Rushdie's phrase. See the English PEN press release of 31 July 2006.

11 Suroor, '"Battle of Brick Lane" Fizzles Out'. As I was finishing this book, Monica Ali wrote a considered response to the controversy, on the eve of the film's release – ironically, in the *Guardian*. See 'The Outrage Economy', *Guardian*, 'Review', 13 October 2007, pp. 4–6.

12 Germaine Greer, 'Reality Bites', *Guardian*, 24 July 2006, www.arts.guardian. co.uk/print/0,,329536594–117599,00.html.

13 Salman Rushdie, 'Brickbats Fly Over Brick Lane' (Letters), *Guardian*, 29 July 2006, www.guardian.co.uk/print/0,,329541026–103683,00.html.

14 Greer, 'Reality Bites'.

15 John Singh, 'Brickbats Fly Over Brick Lane' (Letters), *Guardian*, 29 July 2006, www.guardian.co.uk/print/0,,329541026–103683,00.html.

16 Tarquin Hall, *Salaam Brick Lane: A Year in the New East End* (London: John Murray, 2005).

17 This study – *The New East End: Kinship, Race and Conflict*, by Geoff Dench, Kate Gavron and Michael Young (London: Profile Books, 2006) – updates the findings of the influential 1957 study, *Family and Kinship in East London*, by Michael Young and Peter Willmott.

18 Dench, Gavron and Young, *The New East End*, pp. 134, 8, 230, 231, 229.

19 James Proctor, 'New Ethnicities, the Novel, and the Burdens of Representation', in James F. English (ed.), *A Concise Companion to Contemporary British Fiction* (Oxford: Blackwell, 2006), pp. 101–20.

20 Graham Huggan, *The Postcolonial Exotic: Marketing the Margins* (London: Routledge, 2001), pp. vii, viii.

21 Proctor, 'New Ethnicities', pp. 112, 118.

22 Mark Stein, *Black British Literature: Novels of Transformation* (Columbus: Ohio State University Press, 2004), p. 183.

23 Huggan, *The Postcolonial Exotic*, pp. 32–3.

24 Tobias A. Wachinger, *Posing In-between: Postcolonial Englishness and the Commodification of Hybridity* (Frankfurt: Peter Lang, 2003), pp. 2, 6.

25 Timothy Brennan, *At Home in the World: Cosmopolitanism Now* (Cambridge, MA: Harvard University Press, 1997), pp. 1–2, 4.

26 Wachinger, *Posing In-between*, pp. 9, 193, 194, 195, 196.

27 See Dominic Head, *The Cambridge Introduction to Modern British Fiction, 1950–2000* (Cambridge: Cambridge University Press, 2002), pp. 182–3. The reference is to Homi Bhabha's essay 'DissemiNation: Time, Narrative, and the Margins of the Modern Nation', in *Nation and Narration*, ed. by Bhabha (London: Routledge, 1990), pp. 291–322.

28 See, for example, Natasha Walter, 'The Children of Paradise', *Guardian*, 'Review', 3 September 2005, p. 21; and Peter Kemp, 'The Sound and the Fury', *The Sunday Times*, 'Culture', 11 September 2005, pp. 41–2.

29 Peter Kemp suggested that much of *Shalimar the Clown* 'resembles a retirement home for the doddery old clichés of magic realism'. See Kemp, 'The Sound and the Fury', p. 42.

30 Marco Roth, 'Give the People What They Want', *Times Literary Supplement*, 5345, 9 September 2005, pp. 19–20.

31 Jason Cowley, 'From Here to Kashmir', *Observer*, 'Review', 11 September 2005, p. 17.

32 Kwame Anthony Appiah, *The Ethics of Identity* (Princeton, NJ: Princeton University Press, 2005), pp. 256, 257, 258.

33 Appiah, *The Ethics of Identity*, p. 268.

34 Bruce King, *The Internationalization of English Literature*, Oxford English Literary History, vol. 13: 1948–2000 (Oxford: Oxford University Press, 2004), pp. 235–6, 322–4.

Chapter 4   Terrorism in Transatlantic Perspective

1 James Wood, 'Tell Me How Does it Feel?', *Guardian*, 6 October 2001, www.books.guardian.co.uk/departments/generalfiction/story/0,6000,563868,00.html (26.11.01).

2 Jay McInerney, 'Brightness Falls', *Guardian*, 'Saturday', 15 September 2001, pp. 1–2. The novel in question was eventually published as *The Good Life* (London: Bloomsbury, 2006).

3 Wood, 'Tell Me How Does it Feel?'

4 Gerald Isaaman, 'It's a Mad, Mad, World that Inspires Martin', *Camden New Journal*, www.camdennewjournal.co.uk/archives/r301003_6.htm (26.9.06).

5 Martin Amis, 'The Voice of the Lonely Crowd', *Guardian*, 1 June 2002, www.books.guardian.co.uk/print/0,,4425124–99939,00.html (26/9/06).

6 Isaaman, 'It's a Mad, Mad, World'.

7 The invocation of Fielding's *Joseph Andrews* announces several tacit claims: for Amis's continuing development of the comic novel; for an updating of the picaresque; and for an underlying gravity in the treatment of social mores.

8 James Diedrick, *Understanding Martin Amis*, 2nd edn (Columbia: University of South Carolina Press, 2004), p. 280. This important suggestion, squirrelled away in a footnote of the second edition of Diedrick's book, illustrates why the hindsight enjoyed by the critic is needed to build on the work of reviewers.

9 See Robert Douglas-Fairhurst, 'Dickens With a Snarl', *Observer*, 'Review', 24 August 2003, p. 15.

10 Martin Amis, 'The Age of Horrorism: Faith and the Dependent Mind', *Observer*, 'Review', 10 September 2006, pp. 4–7, 9–10.

11 Amis, 'The Voice of the Lonely Crowd'.

12   Martin Amis, 'Fear and Loathing', *Guardian*, 18 September 2001, www.guardian. co.uk/print/0,,4259170–108926,00.html (26/09/2006).

13   The publication of Amis's *The Second Plane* (London: Jonathan Cape, 2008) was announced as the copy-editing of this book was being completed.

14   Douglas-Fairhurst, 'Dickens With a Snarl'.

15   Emma Brockes, 'Even the Praise is Bad for You', *Guardian*, 29 August 2003, www.books.guardian.co.uk/print/0,,4742651–99930,00.html (26.9.06)

16   Kate Muir, 'Amis Needs a Drink', *The Times*, 13 September 2006, martinamisweb. com/interviews_files/muir_interviews.doc (26.9.06). James Diedrick records the same observation in an interview Amis gave Mark Lawson for *Front Row* (BBC 4, 1 September 2001). See *Understanding Martin Amis*, 2nd edn, p. 279.

17   Terry Eagleton, *Holy Terror* (Oxford: Oxford University Press, 2005), pp. 1–2, vi.

18   Peter Conradi, *Fyodor Dostoevsky* (Basingstoke: Macmillan, 1988), p. 99.

19   Eagleton, *Holy Terror*, pp. 56, 91–2. Joseph Conrad, *The Secret Agent*, ed. Bruce Harkness and S. W. Reid, 'The Cambridge Edition of the Works of Joseph Conrad' (Cambridge: Cambridge University Press, 1990), pp. 30, 33.

20   Eagleton, *Holy Terror*, pp. 121, 100, 121–3, 124, 125, 126, 127.

21   Alex Houen, *Terrorism and Modern Literature, from Joseph Conrad to Ciaran Carson* (Oxford: Oxford University Press, 2002), pp. 35, 36.

22   Elaine B. Safer, *Mocking the Age: The Later Novels of Philip Roth* (Albany: State University of New York Press, 2006), p. 80.

23   I am in agreement, here, with Safer, who sees in the business of glove-making, the embodiment of 'social and ethnic characteristics of American citizens whose ethics and outlook are different from the careless violence of Merry Levov and her friends.' See *Mocking the Age*, p. 86.

24   Safer, *Mocking the Age*, p. 86.

25   Mark Shechner, *Up Society's Ass, Copper: Rereading Philip Roth* (Madison: University of Wisconsin Press, 2003), p. 160.

26   Frank Kermode, *Pleasing Myself: From 'Beowulf' to Philip Roth* (London: Allen Lane, 2001), p. 256.

27   Safer, *Mocking the Age*, p. 93.

28   Stephen Abell, 'Ahmad's America', *Times Literary Supplement*, 5391, 28 July 2006, pp. 21–2.

29   Jem Poster, 'Paradise Lost', *Guardian*, 'Review', 5 August 2006, p. 14.

30   Stephen Amidon, 'America's Worst Nightmare', *The Sunday Times*, 'Culture', 6 August 2006, p. 42.

31   See, for example, Tim Adams, 'Portrait of the Terrorist as a Young Aesthete', *Observer*, 'Review', 23 July 2006, p. 24.

32   Thomas Jones, 'Mr Down-by-the-Levee', *London Review of Books*, 28: 17, 7 September 2006, pp. 29–30.

33   Martin Amis, 'The Last Days of Muhammad Atta', *Observer*, 'Magazine', 3 September 2006, pp. 16–17, 19, 21, 23, 25–6, 28.

34 Amis, 'The Age of Horrorism', p. 7.
35 Amis, 'The Last Days of Muhammad Atta', p. 28.
36 Amis, 'The Age of Horrorism', p. 10. See Joseph Conrad, *'The Shadow-Line' and 'Within the Tides'*, Collected Edition (London: Dent, 1950), pp. v–vi.
37 As I was completing this book, a public spat between Eagleton and Amis, now both professors at the University of Manchester, was running its course, with Eagleton accusing Amis of Islamophobia, and Amis rearticulating his agonistic views, but retrenching from the stance he had taken in a previous interview. (See, for example, 'Enough says Amis in Eagleton feud', *Guardian*, 13 October 2007, p. 18.) The interesting question is whether or not such spats are propitious for advancing a more public role for English studies, or whether (as I am inclined to think) the media noise of personality and confrontation, which makes such events newsworthy, silences the substantive debate.
38 'Only Love and Then Oblivion. Love Was All They Had to Set Against Their Murderers', front-page article, *Guardian*, 15 September 2001.
39 'Beyond Belief', *Guardian*, 'G2', 12 September 2001, p. 2.
40 John Banville, 'A Day in the Life', review of *Saturday*, *New York Review of Books*, 52: 9, 26 May 2005, www.nybooks.com/articles/17993 (20.10.2005).
41 Ian McEwan 'Faith v Fact', *Guardian*, 7 January 2005, 'G2', p. 6.

Chapter 5   Global Futures: Novelists, Critics, Citizens

1 Elaine Showalter thinks Roux 'sounds a lot like Julia Kristeva'. See *Faculty Towers: The Academic Novel and Its Discontents* (Philadelphia: University of Pennsylvania Press, 2005), p. 106.
2 As in *American Pastoral*, the story is pieced together by narrator Nathan Zuckerman, though here Roth is at greater pains to downplay the sense of speculation, and to explain how the testimony from which the story is built reaches Zuckerman.
3 '11 September: Some *LRB* Writers Reflect on the Reasons and Consequences', *London Review of Books*, 23: 19, 4 October 2001, pp. 20–5.
4 Marjorie Perloff's letter was published in *London Review of Books*, 23: 20, 18 October 2001, p. 4.
5 McQuail observes that 'out of 29 pieces, 14 were datelined in the USA, 11 in Europe and 4 elsewhere.' See *London Review of Books*, 23: 23, 29 November 2001, p. 4.
6 '11 September: Some *LRB* Writers Reflect on the Reasons and Consequences', pp. 21, 25.
7 '11 September: Some *LRB* Writers Reflect on the Reasons and Consequences', p. 23.
8 For Jean Baudrillard's comparable, but more philosophical reflections on the events of 11 September 2001, see *'The Spirit of Terrorism' and 'Requiem for the*

Twin Towers', trans, Chris Turner (London: Verso, 2002). Baudrillard suggest that the attacks on the World Trade Centre constitute 'the absolute event, the "mother" of all events, the pure event uniting within itself all the events that have never taken place' (p. 4).

9 James Wood, 'Tell Me How Does it Feel?', *Guardian*, 6 October 2001, www. books.guardian.co.uk/departments/generalfiction/story/0,6000,563868,00. html (26.11.01).

10 The image in question is a photograph taken by Richard Drew. Tim Junod's story about it, and the possible identity of the falling man, appeared in the September 2003 issue of *Esquire* magazine. A documentary, *9/11: The Falling Man* was subsequently made by Henry Singer and Richard Numeroff, and first screened in March 2006 (on Channel 4).

11 Daniel Soar, 'Bile, Blood, Bilge, Mulch', *London Review of Books*, 29: 1, 4 January 2007, pp. 14–17.

12 Martin Amis, 'The Age of Horrorism: Faith and the Dependent Mind', *Observer*, 'Review', 10 September 2006, pp. 4–7, 9–10.

13 Ed Husain, *The Islamist: Why I Joined Radical Islam in Britain, What I Saw Inside and Why I Left* (London: Penguin, 2007), pp. 282, 54, 284.

14 Christine Sypnowich, 'Cosmopolitans, Cosmopolitanism, and Human Flourishing', in Gillian Brock and Harry Brighouse (eds), *The Political Philosophy of Cosmopolitanism* (Cambridge: Cambridge University Press, 2005), pp. 55–74.

15 Gillian Brock and Harry Brighouse, 'Introduction' to *The Political Philosophy of Cosmopolitanism*, p. 3.

16 Brock and Brighouse, 'Introduction' to *The Political Philosophy of Cosmopolitanism*, p. 3.

17 Kok-Chor Tan, 'The Demands of Justice and National Allegiances', in Gillian Brock and Harry Brighouse (eds), *The Political Philosophy of Cosmopolitanism*, pp. 164–79.

18 Ulrich Beck, *Cosmopolitan Vision*, trans. Ciaran Cronin (Cambridge: Polity Press, 2006), pp. 7, 2.

19 Beck, *Cosmopolitan Vision*, pp. 69, 70.

20 There will inevitably be charges of tokenism and idealism levelled against the relationship between Christy, the Irish plumber, and Jasmina, a divorcée from an arranged Hindu marriage. But it is the element of sanguinity about the economic system, signalled in such things as Jasmina's work (as a mortgage adviser, however disillusioned), and Tremain's deployment of the device of the legacy, that will surely dismay academic readers.

21 Kwame Anthony Appiah, *Cosmopolitanism: Ethics in a World of Strangers* (London: Allen Lane, 2006), pp. xv, xviii.

161

Bibliography

Abell, Stephen, 'Ahmad's America', *Times Literary Supplement*, 5391, 28 July 2006, p. 21–2.

Adams, Tim, 'Portrait of the Terrorist as a Young Aesthete', *Observer*, 'Review', 23 July 2006, p. 24.

Ali, Monica, *Brick Lane* (London: Doubleday, 2003).

Ali, Monica, 'The Outrage Economy', *Guardian*, 'Review', 13 October 2007, pp. 4–6.

Amidon, Stephen, 'America's Worst Nightmare', *The Sunday Times*, 'Culture', 6 August 2006, p. 42.

Amis, Kingsley, *Lucky Jim* (Harmondsworth: Penguin, 1992).

Amis, Martin, *Money* (Harmondsworth: Penguin, 1985).

Amis, Martin, *Einstein's Monsters* (London: Jonathan Cape, 1987).

Amis, Martin, 'Fear and Loathing', *Guardian*, 18 September 2001, www.guardian.co.uk/print/0,,4259170–108926,00.html (26/09/2006).

Amis, Martin, *Koba the Dread* (London: Jonathan Cape, 2002).

Amis, Martin, 'The Voice of the Lonely Crowd', *Guardian*, 1 June 2002, www.books.guardian.co.uk/print/0,,4425124–99939,00.html (26/9/06).

Amis, Martin, *Yellow Dog* (London: Jonathan Cape, 2003).

Amis, Martin, *House of Meetings* (London: Jonathan Cape, 2006).

Amis, Martin, 'The Last Days of Muhammad Atta', *Observer*, 'Magazine', 3 September 2006, pp. 16–17, 19, 21, 23, 25–6, 28.

Amis, Martin, 'The Age of Horrorism: Faith and the Dependent Mind', *Observer*, 'Review', 10 September 2006, pp. 4–7, 9–10.

Appiah, Kwame Anthony, *The Ethics of Identity* (Princeton, NJ: Princeton University Press, 2005).

Appiah, Kwame Anthony, *Cosmopolitanism: Ethics in a World of Strangers* (London: Allen Lane, 2006).

Appignanesi, Lisa, 'PEN is Concerned About Protests Over the Filming of Monica Ali's Brick Lane', www.englishpen.org/news/monicaalis bricklane/.

Ballard, J. G., *Crash* (London: Vintage, 1995).

Banville, John, *The Sea* (London: Picador, 2005).

Banville, John, 'A Day in the Life', review of *Saturday*, *New York Review of Books*, 52: 9, 26 May 2005, www.nybooks.com/articles/17993 (20.10.2005).

Barstow, Stan, *A Kind of Loving* (Harmondsworth: Penguin, 1962).

Baudrillard, Jean, *'The Spirit of Terrorism' and 'Requiem for the Twin Towers'*, trans. Chris Turner (London: Verso, 2002).

Beck, Ulrich, *Cosmopolitan Vision*, trans. Ciaran Cronin (Cambridge: Polity Press, 2006).

Benson, Peter, *The Shape of Clouds* (London: Hodder and Stoughton, 1996).

Bentley, Nick, ed., *British Fiction of the 1990s* (London: Routledge, 2005).

Berger, John, *G* (London: Bloomsbury, 1996).

Bhabha, Homi, ed., *Nation and Narration* (London: Routledge, 1990).

Binding, Paul, 'Upwardly-Mobile Men out of Wells', *Times Literary Supplement*, 4969, 26 September 1998, p. 27.

Blanchard, Stephen, *Wilson's Island* (London: Chatto and Windus, 1997).

Blanchard, Stephen, *The Paraffin Child* (London: Chatto and Windus, 1999).

Bloom, Clive, *Literature, Politics and Intellectual Crisis in Britain Today* (Basingstoke: Palgrave, 2001).

Boyce, Frank Cottrell, 'How to be Good', *Guardian*, 'Review', 10 June 2006, p. 16.

Bradbury, Malcolm, ed., *The Novel Today: Contemporary Writers on Modern Fiction*, revd edn (London: Fontana, 1990).

Bradbury, Malcolm, *The Modern British Novel* (London: Secker and Warburg, 1993); revd edn (London: Penguin, 2001).

Braine, John, *Room at the Top* (London: Mandarin, 1996).

Brannigan, John, *Orwell to the Present: Literature in England, 1945–2000* (Basingstoke: Palgrave Macmillan, 2003).

Brennan, Timothy, *At Home in the World: Cosmopolitanism Now* (Cambridge, MA: Harvard University Press, 1997), pp. 1–2.

Brock, Gillian, and Harry Brighouse, eds, *The Political Philosophy of Cosmopolitanism* (Cambridge: Cambridge University Press, 2005).

Brockes, Emma, 'Even the Praise is Bad for You', *Guardian*, 29 August 2003, www.books.guardian.co.uk/print/0,,4742651–99930,00.html (26.9.06).

Brockman, John, *The Third Culture: Beyond the Scientific Revolution* (New York: Simon and Schuster, 1995).

Carey, John, *What Good are the Arts?* (London: Faber and Faber, 2005).

Childs, Peter, *Contemporary Novelists: British Fiction Since 1970* (Basingstoke: Palgrave Macmillan, 2005).

Coetzee, J. M., *Life and Times of Michael K* (Harmondsworth: Penguin, 1985).

Coetzee, J. M., *Disgrace* (London: Secker and Warburg, 1999).

Conrad, Joseph, *'The Shadow-Line' and 'Within the Tides'*, Collected Edition (London: Dent, 1950).

Conrad, Joseph, *The Secret Agent*, ed. Bruce Harkness and S. W. Reid (Cambridge: Cambridge University Press, 1990).

Conradi, Peter, *Fyodor Dostoevsky* (Basingstoke: Macmillan, 1988).

Cowan, Andrew, *Crustaceans* (London: Hodder and Stoughton, 2000).

Cowley, Jason, 'From Here to Kashmir', *Observer*, 'Review', 11 September 2005, p. 17.

Dabydeen, David, *A Harlot's Progress* (London: Jonathan Cape, 1999).

DeLillo, Don, *Mao II* (London: Vintage, 1992).

DeLillo, Don, *Falling Man* (London: Picador, 2007).

Dench, Geoff, Kate Gavron and Michael Young, *The New East End: Kinship, Race and Conflict* (London: Profile Books, 2006).

Desai, Kiran, *The Inheritance of Loss* (London: Hamish Hamilton, 2006).

Diedrick, James, *Understanding Martin Amis*, 2nd edn (Columbia: University of South Carolina Press, 2004).

Dostoevsky, Fyodor, *Demons* [*The Devils*], trans. Richard Pevear and Larissa Volokhonsky (London: Vintage, 1994).

Douglas-Fairhurst, Robert, 'Dickens With a Snarl', *Observer*, 'Review', 24 August 2003, p. 15.

Drabble, Margaret, *The Radiant Way* (Harmondsworth: Penguin, 1988).

Drabble, Margaret, *A Natural Curiosity* (Harmondsworth: Penguin, 1990).

Drabble, Margaret, *The Gates of Ivory* (Harmondsworth: Penguin, 1992).

Eagleton, Terry, *Holy Terror* (Oxford: Oxford University Press, 2005).

Emecheta, Buchi, *Second-Class Citizen* (Oxford: Heinemann, 1994).

English, James F., *The Economy of Prestige: Prizes, Awards, and the Circulation of Cultural Value* (Cambridge, MA: Harvard University Press, 2005).

English, James F., ed., *A Concise Companion to Contemporary British Fiction* (Oxford: Blackwell, 2006).

Farrell, J. G., *The Siege of Krishnapur* (London: Weidenfeld and Nicolson, 1973).

Bibliography

Foer, Jonathan Safran, *Extremely Loud and Incredibly Close* (London: Hamish Hamilton, 2005).

Fowles, John, *The French Lieutenant's Woman* (London: Pan, 1987).

Fowles, John, *The Ebony Tower* (London: Pan, 1986).

Frow, John, *Cultural Studies and Cultural Value* (Oxford: Oxford University Press, 1995).

Gasiorek, Andrzej, *Post-War British Fiction: Realism and After* (London: Edward Arnold, 1995).

Gavron, Jeremy, *An Acre of Barren Ground* (London: Simon and Schuster, 2005).

Gordimer, Nadine, *The Conservationist* (London: Jonathan Cape, 1974).

Greacen, Lavinia, J. G. *Farrell: The Making of a Writer* (London: Bloomsbury, 1999).

Greene, Graham, *Brighton Rock* (Harmondsworth: Penguin, 1980).

Greer, Germaine, 'Reality Bites', *Guardian*, 24 July 2006, www.arts.guardian. co.uk/print/0,,329536594–117599,00.html.

Grylls, David, 'Not Waving but Drowning', *The Sunday Times*, 'Culture', 12 June 2005, p. 53.

Hall, Tarquin, *Salaam Brick Lane: A Year in the New East End* (London: John Murray, 2005).

Halliday, Fred, *Two Hours That Shook the World, September 11, 2001: Causes and Consequences* (London: Saqi Books, 2002).

Hamid, Mohsin, *The Reluctant Fundamentalist* (London: Hamish Hamilton, 2007).

Head, Dominic, *The Cambridge Introduction to Modern British Fiction, 1950–2000* (Cambridge: Cambridge University Press, 2002).

Homes, A. M., *The End of Alice* (London: Granta Books, 2006).

Homes, A. M., *This Book Will Save Your Life* (London: Granta Books, 2006).

Hopkins, David, *After Modern Art: 1945–2000* (Oxford: Oxford University Press, 2000).

Hornby, Nick, *High Fidelity: A Novel* (London: Victor Gollanncz, 1995).

Hornby, Nick, *How to be Good* (London: Viking, 2001).

Hornby, Nick, *A Long Way Down* (London: Viking, 2005).

Hornby, Nick, *The Complete Polysyllabic Spree* (London: Viking, 2006).

Houen, Alex, *Terrorism and Modern Literature, from Joseph Conrad to Ciaran Carson* (Oxford: Oxford University Press, 2002).

Huggan, Graham, *The Postcolonial Exotic: Marketing the Margins* (London: Routledge, 2001).

Husain, Ed, *The Islamist: Why I Joined Radical Islam in Britain, What I Saw Inside and Why I Left* (Harmondsworth: Penguin, 2007).

Innes, C. L., *A History of Black and Asian Writing in Britain, 1700—2000* (Cambridge: Cambridge University Press, 2002).

Isaaman, Gerald, 'It's a Mad, Mad, World that Inspires Martin', *Camden New Journal*, www.camdennewjournal.co.uk/archives/r301003_6.htm (26.9.06).

Ishiguro, Kazuo, *Never Let Me Go* (London: Faber and Faber, 2005).

Jack, Ian, 'It's Only a Novel', *Guardian*, 'Review', 20 December 2003, p. 7.

Jensen, Hal, 'All Endeavour Useless', *Times Literary Supplement*, 5374, 31 March 2004, p. 20.

Jones, Thomas, 'Mr Down-by-the-Levee', *London Review of Books*, 28: 17, 7 September 2006, pp. 29–30.

Kemp, Peter, 'The Sound and the Fury', *The Sunday Times*, 'Culture', 11 September 2005, pp. 41–2.

Kermode, Frank, *Pleasing Myself: From 'Beowulf' to Philip Roth* (London: Allen Lane, 2001).

King, Bruce, *V. S. Naipaul*, 2nd edn (Basingstoke: Palgrave Macmillan, 2003).

King, Bruce, *The Internationalization of English Literature*, Oxford English Literary History, vol. 13: 1948–2000 (Oxford: Oxford University Press, 2004).

Lea, Daniel, *Graham Swift* (Manchester: Manchester University Press, 2005).

Lea, Richard, 'Local Protests Over Brick Lane Film', *Guardian*, Monday 17 July 2006, www.books.guardian.co.uk/print/0,,329531826–99819,00.html.

Lea, Richard, 'Novelists Hit Back at Brick Lane Protestors', *Guardian*, 31 July 2006, www.books.guardian.co.uk/print/0,,329542510–99819,00.html.

Levine, Norman, *From a Seaside Town* (Erin, Ontario: Porcupine's Quill, 1993).

Lewis, Trevor, 'At a Glance' [untitled short review], *The Sunday Times*, 'Culture', 25 June 2006, p. 55.

Lezard, Nicholas, 'Morality Bites', *Guardian*, 'Saturday Review', 24 April 1999, p. 11.

Liddle, Rod, 'Comment', *The Sunday Times*, 'Culture', 14 January 2007, pp. 6–7.

LRB symposium, '11 September: Some *LRB* Writers Reflect on the Reasons and Consequences', *London Review of Books*, 23: 19, 4 October 2001, pp. 20–5.

McCrum, Robert, 'The Human Factor', *Observer*, 'Review', 27 May 2001, p. 15.

McEwan, Ian, *The Child in Time* (London: Jonathan Cape, 1987).

McEwan, Ian, *Black Dogs* (London: Picador, 1993).

McEwan, Ian, *The Comfort of Strangers* (London: Vintage, 1997).

McEwan, Ian, *Enduring Love* (London: Jonathan Cape, 1997).

McEwan, Ian, *Amsterdam* (London: Jonathan Cape, 1998).

McEwan, Ian, 'Beyond Belief', *Guardian*, 'G2', 12 September 2001, p. 2.

McEwan, Ian, 'Only Love and Then Oblivion. Love Was All They Had to Set Against Their Murderers', front-page article, *Guardian*, 15 September 2001.

McEwan, Ian, 'Faith v Fact', *Guardian*, 'G2', 7 January 2005, p. 6.

McEwan, Ian, *Saturday* (London: Jonathan Cape, 2005).

McEwan, Ian, *On Chesil Beach* (London: Jonathan Cape, 2007).

Macfarlane, Robert, 'The World at Arm's Length', *Times Literary Supplement*, 5331, 3 June 2005, p. 19.

McInerney, Jay, 'Brightness Falls', *Guardian*, 'Saturday', 15 September 2001, pp. 1–2.

McInerney, Jay, *The Good Life* (London: Bloomsbury, 2006).

Martin, S. I., *Incomparable World* (New York: George Braziller, 1998).

Messud, Claire, *The Emperor's Children* (London: Picador, 2006).

Middleton, Stanley, *Holiday* (Nottingham: Five Leaves, 1999).

Middleton, Stanley, *Small Change* (London: Hutchinson, 2000).

Middleton, Stanley, *Sterner Stuff* (London: Hutchinson, 2005).

Morrison, Jago, *Contemporary Fiction* (London: Routledge, 2003).

Mudford, Peter, *Graham Greene* (Plymouth: Northcote House, 1996).

Muir, Kate, 'Amis Needs a Drink', *The Times*, 13 September 2006, martinamisweb.com/interviews_files/muir_interviews.doc (26.9.06).

Murdoch, Iris, *The Black Prince* (Harmondsworth: Penguin, 1975).

Murdoch, Iris, *The Sea, The Sea* (Harmondsworth: Penguin, 1980).

Murdoch, Iris, 'Against Dryness: A Polemical Sketch', in *The Novel Today: Contemporary Writers on Modern Fiction*, revd edn, ed. Malcolm Bradbury (London: Fontana, 1990), pp. 15–24.

Mustafa, Fawzia, *V. S. Naipaul* (Cambridge: Cambridge University Press, 1995).

Naipaul, V. S., *'The Return of Eva Perón' and 'The Killings in Trinidad'* (Harmondsworth: Penguin, 1981).

Naipaul, V. S., *In A Free State* (London: Picador, 2002).

167

Naipaul, V. S., *A Bend in the River* (London: Picador, 2002).

O'Brien, Sean, 'Toppers' Talk', *Times Literary Supplement*, 5327, 6 May 2005, p. 20.

Olin, Jessica, 'Feral Chihuahuas', *London Review of Books*, 28: 12, 22 June 2006, pp. 13–14.

Paling, Chris, *Deserters* (London: Jonathan Cape, 1996).

Paling, Chris, *A Town by the Sea* (London: Jonathan Cape, 2005).

Phillips, Adam, 'My Own Ghost', *London Review of Books*, 27: 15, 4 August 2005, pp. 35–6.

Poster, Jem, 'Paradise Lost', *Guardian*, 'Review', 5 August 2006, p. 14.

Proctor, James, 'New Ethnicities, the Novel, and the Burdens of Representation', in *A Concise Companion to Contemporary British Fiction*, ed. James F. English (Oxford: Blackwell, 2006), pp. 101–20.

Robbins, Bruce, *Secular Vocations: Intellectuals, Professionalism, Culture* (London: Verso, 1993).

Roth, Marco, 'Give the People What They Want', *Times Literary Supplement*, 5345, 9 September 2005, pp. 19–20.

Roth, Philip, *American Pastoral* (London: Vintage, 2005).

Roth, Philip, *The Human Stain* (London: Vintage, 2005).

Rubin Rabinovitz, *The Reaction Against Experiment in the English Novel, 1950–1960* (New York: Columbia University Press, 1967).

Rushdie, Salman, *Midnight's Children* (London: Picador, 1982).

Rushdie, Salman, *Shame* (London: Picador, 1984).

Rushdie, Salman, *Shalimar the Clown* (London: Jonathan Cape, 2005).

Rushdie, Salman, 'Brickbats Fly Over Brick Lane' (Letters), *Guardian*, 29 July 2006, www.guardian.co.uk/print/0,,329541026–103683,00.html.

Safer, Elaine B., *Mocking the Age: The Later Novels of Philip Roth* (Albany: State University of New York Press, 2006), p. 80.

Sansom, Ian, 'Emotional Sushi', *London Review of Books*, 23: 15, 9 August 2001, pp. 19–20.

Sansom, Ian, 'His Own Peak', *London Review of Books*, 26: 9, 6 May 2004, pp. 32–3.

Sayer, Paul, *The God Child* (London: Bloomsbury, 1996).

Scott, Paul, *Staying On* (London: Arrow, 1997).

Selvon, Sam, *The Lonely Londoners* (Harlow: Longman, 1998).

Shaffer, Brian W., *Reading the Novel in English, 1950–2000* (Oxford: Blackwell, 2006).

Bibliography

Shechner, Mark, *Up Society's Ass, Copper: Rereading Philip Roth* (Madison: University of Wisconsin Press, 2003).

Showalter, Elaine, *Faculty Towers: The Academic Novel and Its Discontents* (Philadelphia: University of Pennsylvania Press, 2005).

Singh, John, 'Brickbats Fly Over Brick Lane' (Letters), *Guardian*, 29 July 2006, www.guardian.co.uk/print/0,,329541026–103683,00.html.

Smith, Norman, *Bad Friday* (London: New Beacon Books, 1985).

Smith, Zadie, *White Teeth* (London: Hamish Hamilton, 2000).

Smith, Zadie, *On Beauty* (London: Hamish Hamilton, 2005).

Soar, Daniel, 'Bile, Blood, Bilge, Mulch', *London Review of Books*, 29: 1, 4 January 2007, pp. 14–17.

Stein, Mark, *Black British Literature: Novels of Transformation* (Columbus: Ohio State University Press, 2004), p. 183.

Suroor, Hasan, ' "Battle of Brick Lane" Fizzles Out', *The Hindu*, 2 August 2006, www.hinduonnet.com/thehindu/thscrip/print.pl?file=2006080 205071100. htm&date=2006/08/02/&prd=th&.

Swift, Graham, *Last Orders* (London: Picador, 1996).

Swift, Graham, *Tomorrow* (London: Picador, 2007).

Sypnowich, Christine, 'Cosmopolitans, Cosmopolitanism, and Human Flourishing', in *The Political Philosophy of Cosmopolitanism*, ed. Gillian Brock and Harry Brighouse (Cambridge: Cambridge University Press, 2005), pp. 55–74.

Tan, Kok-Chor, 'The Demands of Justice and National Allegiances', in *The Political Philosophy of Cosmopolitanism*, ed. Gillian Brock and Harry Brighouse (Cambridge: Cambridge University Press, 2005), pp. 164–79.

Taylor, D. J., *Trespass* (London: Anchor, 1999).

Todd, Richard, *Consuming Fictions: The Booker Prize and Fiction in Britain Today* (London: Bloomsbury, 1996).

Tremain, Rose, *The Road Home* (London: Chatto and Windus, 2007).

Updike, John, *Terrorist* (London: Hamish Hamilton, 2006).

Wachinger, Tobias A., *Posing In-between: Postcolonial Englishness and the Commodification of Hybridity* (Frankfurt: Peter Lang, 2003).

Walter, Natasha, 'The Children of Paradise', *Guardian*, 'Review', 3 September 2005, p. 21.

Walton, John K., *The British Seaside: Holidays and Resorts in the Twentieth Century* (Manchester: Manchester University Press, 2000).

Waters, Juliet, 'The Little Chill: Has the Booker Prize Chosen the Noveau Beaujolais of Fiction?', www.montrealmirror.com/ARCHIVES/1998/120398/book.html (13.7.05).

Williams, Raymond, *Politics and Letters: Interviews with 'New Left Review'* (London: New Left Books, 1979).

Williams, Raymond, *Writing in Society* (London: Verso, 1983).

Williams, Raymond, *Border Country* (London: Hogarth Press, 1988).

Wolff, Tobias, *The Night in Question* (London: Bloomsbury, 1996).

Wood, James, 'Tell Me How Does it Feel?', *Guardian*, 6 October 2001, www.books.guardian.co.uk/departments/generalfiction/story/0,6000,563868,00.html (26.11.01).

Index

Index